Preaching Better

PREACHING BETTER

Frank J. McNulty,
editor

PAULIST PRESS
New York/Mahwah

The publisher gratefully acknowledges the use of excerpts from Elisabeth Schüssler Fiorenza's article in *A New Look at Preaching* published by Michael Glazier, Inc. Used with permission.

Copyright © 1985 by
Frank J. McNulty

All rights reserved. No part of this book may be reproduced or transmitted in any form or by any means, electronic or mechanical, including photocopying, recording, or by any information storage and retrieval system without permission in writing from the publisher.

Library of Congress
Catalog Card Number: 84–61976

ISBN: 0–8091–2682–6

Published by Paulist Press
997 Macarthur Boulevard
Mahwah, N.J. 07430

Printed and bound in the United States of America

CONTENTS

FOREWORD   1

INTRODUCTION: THE GOOD EYE   3

Part I: Lights

A PREACHER'S NOTEBOOK—
PERSONAL RESOURCE CENTER
Robert F. Morneau   17

THOUGHTS ON STORYTELLING
Jay O'Callaghan   30

THE LECTIONARY: TOO MUCH OF A GOOD THING?
William Skudlarek, O.S.B.   37

USING LITERATURE
James C. Turro   45

THE SILENCED MAJORITY
NEEDS TO COME TO WORD
Elisabeth Schüssler Fiorenza   51

Part II: Camera

PSYCHOLOGICAL PERSPECTIVE
Neil Mahoney   63

TOUCHING PEOPLE'S HEARTS
Patricia Hickman Livingston   72

UNLOCKING THE IMAGINATION
Fred A. Baumer   80

THE RIGHT BRAIN LANGUAGE OF POWER
Clarence Thomson   87

Part III: Action

TO LIVE THE WORD WITH LITTLE FOLKS
Francis T. Cancro   97

HOW TO PREACH TO ADOLESCENTS
Kieran Sawyer, S.S.N.D.   105

PREACHING TO THE LIVING AT A FUNERAL
Charles Hudson   114

HAVE PATIENCE—
WE'LL BE IN ST. CROIX TONIGHT
John W. Conway   122

*Dedicated to my students
from whom I've learned so much,
especially those at Darlington, Fordham and St. Norbert*

FOREWORD

When a director is ready to shoot a film, he shouts "lights" and at his word large floodlights are turned on to brighten up the set. We call the first section "lights" because it is a preparatory phase in preaching, a shining of lights on certain parts of our world. Robert Morneau outlines a system for organizing material; Jay O'Callaghan affirms the value of storytelling; William Skudlarek advises on the proper use of Scripture; James Turro argues a case for the preacher using literature. In the final chapter of this section, Elisabeth Schüssler Fiorenza reminds the homilist that to be effective the voices of women should be heard.

Next, the director calls for "camera" and the operators move them to places where they can shoot the scene. Just as a camera focuses and takes aim, so does a preacher. In this second section Neil Mahoney writes of the psychology of preacher and hearer; Pat Livingston urges that some of the message be directed to the heart; Fred Baumer reminds us of the role of imagination; Clarence Thomson makes good use of recent research on how the brain works in communication.

"Action" is the final word the director uses as a signal to begin. In the third and final section, the book speaks in practical terms of the preaching endeavor. All of what has been covered already will help the daily or Sunday homily. Here the authors offer advice for special occasions. Frank Cancro suggests guidelines for reaching children; Kieran Sawyer speaks of the adolescent hearer of the word; Charles Hudson and John Conway advise the preacher on two frequent situations: the funeral and the wedding.

INTRODUCTION: THE GOOD EYE

Sometimes a comedy manages to give an insightful message while it makes us laugh. This could be said of *A Thousand Clowns,* a play by Herb Gardner. This popular play and movie told the story of Murray Burns, a delightful non-conformist, and his relationship with his nephew Nick. They were a mutual admiration society and in one scene the uncle sings the praises of the young boy:

> The kid was the best straight man I ever had. He is a laugher and laughers are rare. I mean, you tell that kid something funny, not just any piece of corn but something funny, and he'll give you your money's worth. It's not just funny jokes he reads or I tell him that he laughs at. Not just set up funny stuff. He sees street jokes, he has the good eye, he sees subway farce and cartoon humor and all the cartoons people make by being alive. He had a good eye!

What pleases Murray so much is the boy's sense of humor. My guess is that Nick's good eye helps him to become not merely a laugher but an astute and sensitive observer of life. He can see the cartoons people make by being alive. He has a gift, a feel, a touch, an instinct some people lack.

On a busy corner one beggar was getting more money than

others in the same area. People were moved by a sign he carried: "It's April and I'm blind." Even those of us who are not physically blind sometimes fail to appreciate fully the beauty of April. We lack what Nick has: the good eye. The beauty of nature, the wonder of life, the fascination of people—it's all there for our noticing, enjoying, feeling and sharing, but there are times when we put our heads down, cast our eyes to the ground or our noses to the grindstone and see nothing. We might as well be blind. This could become a disastrous handicap for anyone but especially for the preacher.

On the other hand, the person who has a good eye has an ability that could be an invaluable asset for the preacher. This is so because of the nature of the preaching endeavor. At the Eucharist, people and priest have come to hear the Word and to break the bread. They gather together from separate places, with different life experiences, and each person brings a story special and unique. All those stories meet the Jesus story, his life, death and resurrection. When the preacher has a good eye, his homily will not only speak the divine story, but will also say something about all those human stories. His good eye will help him to see what needs to be seen and then he will know what needs to be said. He will not know every story in detailed fashion but he will evidence a feel for the pain, joy, doubt, fear, confusion and hope of the people gathered in that congregation. The message will be helping to make sense of life, so it will be interesting, practical, and at times even exciting. Sometimes the good eye will even make it possible to look into hearts and help the homilist to address the concerns he finds there. When all this happens or even some of it, his parishioners will return to their homes and day to day living with more than the parish bulletin.

There is help available for the preacher who appreciates the value of a good eye. Our world has an abundance of artists. These are sensitive and aware people who in one way or another com-

INTRODUCTION: THE GOOD EYE   5

ment on the human condition. For the preachers of the world, they can become helpful allies.

Charles Rice in *New Catholic World* says it this way: "Culture and the arts are sometimes used as synonyms. If culture is all mankind has done, made and managed to communicate to us and if the artist is especially competent in apprehending and expressing that, then we easily come to think of the arts as culture itself. Playwrights and novelists, poets and filmmakers, painters and sculptors, are often telling the story of our times long before sociologists, journalists, and preachers have sufficient language to articulate what we recognize."

Artists can be helpful to the preacher in two ways: as source or model. As source they provide a fund of material for illustrations, comparisons, motivation and often powerful lessons. Of even more importance to the preacher is the modeling. When we meet them through their work, they illustrate clearly for us the process of seeing something important and telling others about it.

Stephen King did this for me in his best seller *Different Seasons*. The passage which struck me most occurs in "The Body," a first person account of young boys searching for the body of another boy who had been killed by a train. They finally find him, and the author is shocked by the fact that the train had "knocked him out of his Keds just as surely as it had knocked the life out of his body." Here is the passage: a stark reflection on the death of one boy by another who happens to be his age!

> That finally rammed it all the way home for me. The kid was dead. The kid wasn't going to get up in the morning anymore or get the runs from eating too many apples or catch poison ivy or wear out the eraser on his Ticonderoga No. 2 during a hard math test . . . the kid wasn't going to give a bloody nose or get one. The kid wasn't, can't, don't, won't, never, shouldn't, couldn't, wouldn't . . . He was the wastebasket

by the teacher's desk, which always smells of wood shavings from the sharpener and dead orange peels from lunch. The haunted house outside of town where the windows are crashed out, the no-trespassing signs away from the fields, the attic full of bats, the cellar full of rats. The kid was dead mister, ma'am, young sir, little miss. The kid was dead.

This passage is in my file. Someday it may become a source for me; the occasion may come when I will quote it. But even if that moment never comes, Stephen King has educated the preacher in me and has done some valuable modeling. In vivid language, full of metaphor and color, he described what "dead" means to one young man. He also tapped into memory and helped me smell again the wastebasket by the teacher's desk. And his description of boyhood things surfaced some nostalgia for other days and personal adventures. One day I might do some of that for people in a homily. It was only one passage in one novel, but the artist can become a friendly ally for those of us who would become better preachers.

The artist is source and model for the preacher but there is even deeper dimension to the help he gives. The playwright and movie maker provide a good example. Because they do it so well they offer to the preacher a reflection on life by weaving before his eyes a story about human beings. It could be reality or fantasy, biography or whimsy, comedy or tragedy, but when it works, the audience gets swept up. Should the preacher be sitting there, he could leave with much more than he had when he came: more ideas, more insights, more convictions, and maybe even more dreams. Stage, movie screen and homily deal with much of the same reality—human relationships, success and failure, good and evil, heroes and villains.

Recently I saw a revival of *A View from the Bridge* by Arthur Miller. He sets this modern tragedy in the Brooklyn waterfront district. Eddie Carbone, the main character, is a longshoreman

INTRODUCTION: THE GOOD EYE 7

who generously raised his dead sister-in-law's child. She has grown into a beautiful young woman when his relationship with her becomes threatened. Eddie has hidden in his apartment two illegal aliens, and the niece falls in love with one of them. Alfieri, the respected neighborhood attorney, advises Eddie to allow his niece to grow up, fall in love and leave his home. Driven by jealousy, he ignores the advice and instead turns in the aliens to the authorities, who arrest them. His action loses for him what he treasured most, the love of his niece and the respect of his friends. Eddie Carbone suffers total humiliation and is finally killed by one of the aliens. A speech by Alfieri is the final one before the curtain falls.

> Most of the time we settle for half and I like it better. But the truth is holy, and even as I know how wrong he was, and his death useless, I tremble, for I confess that something perversely pure calls to me from his memory—not purely good, but himself purely, for he allowed himself to be wholly known and for that I think I will love him more than all my sensible clients. And yet, it is better to settle for half, it must be! And so I mourn him—I admit it—with a certain . . . alarm.

From that stage Arthur Miller touched and spoke to the preacher in me. He said some significant things about life among people who live in Brooklyn and work on the docks but also about people everywhere. And he did more, because his play set off in me a whole series of reflections about the complex nature of the redemptive process. For me, Arthur Miller became source because I may one day speak of Eddie Carbone in a homily. He became model because he told the story so skillfully. The bonus was that he also forced me to reflect on the human endeavor, and the place of Jesus Christ in it. Once again a preacher was helped by someone with a good eye.

Another resource for the preacher is poetry. Webster defines the poet as "someone endowed with great imaginative, emotional or intuitive powers, capable of expressing passions and intuitions in appropriate language." Because of imaginative power, an old boarded up house along the Erie railroad tracks becomes *A House With Nobody In It*. Others looked and saw something useless, even ugly. Joyce Kilmer looked and saw what should have been and once was: a home full of life and love. Because of emotional power the poet can write of his or her own feelings and stir up similar feelings in others. Because of intuitive power, celebration comes easy for the poet and the resulting poem can get us to pause, look, smile, and make some ordinary event a happening.

Gordon Gilsdorf is a poet who did that for me on my fiftieth birthday. This Green Bay priest, in his *On Being Fifty,* picked up my spirits. He reminded me that "wines grow bitter with age or better." He writes that "fifty is a vintage year, the best: sunshine and rain enough, the perfect grape." He took a life experience, spoke of it in concrete images and stirring rhythms and thus made it even more significant. The poet walks through life with us and makes that journey more enjoyable and vivid. So should the preacher. Because of the good eye, the poet puts warmth and living color into moments that at times can seem drab. So should the preacher.

The poet is a natural model for the preacher but becomes source as well when some poems find their way into the homily. I say some because there is great, moving, profound, poetry totally unsuitable. Such poetry needs to be read, reflected upon and read again, before it can be understood. One of these reflective poems would lose the average congregation somewhere during the first stanza. Other poems are quite suitable for use in preaching because they are short, crisp, simple and can usually be grasped in one hearing.

Andrew Costello writes the kind of poetry that, in my thinking, fits into the homily context very well. One of his could serve as an example. Costello calls it "Advice" and it nicely fits any theme that has to do with personal responsibility.

ADVICE

At times we all feel stuck
    and small and all alone,
    caught in a pool of stagnation,
    of stupidity,
    because of sex,
    or money
    or parents,
    or spouse,
    or people at work,
    or something we can't even describe.
And at times we all start looking around us,
    for a way out,
    for the right person,
    to yell to for help,
    someone on the solid ground
    around the grassy edge
    of the pool of stagnation,
    someone who will listen,
    someone who will understand,
    someone who will put everything all right,
    The Outsider.
So we call to the Clergy,
    the Psychologist,
    the Best Friend,
    somebody in the family,
    anybody who will give us a hand
    and lift us out of the pool of stagnation.
Sometimes these help.
Sometimes people even turn to God.

> But then as the days slip by,
>> as I find myself
>> sliding back into the pool of stagnation,
>> I begin to realize
>> that decisions are up to me,
>> that yes I have to work
>> with the love,
>> and grace,
>> the advice of others.
> But I'm the one in charge of my life,
>> the Insider.

One of the reasons why poetry makes easy entry into preaching is that in many ways poets resemble saints. Thornton Wilder puts this reasoning into the words of the narrator/stage manager in his classic *Our Town*. Recall how the disappointed heroine Emily is saddened when she returns to earth to relive her twelfth birthday. She is saddened because her parents suffer from the blindness we mentioned earlier that comes when people forget to look up from the grindstone. She asks the stage manager: "Do any human beings ever realize life while they live it, every, every minute?" He answers quietly "No-o, saints and poets maybe, they do some."

Part of realizing life is having the good eye, but saints do not seem to be as readily available to the preacher as poets. That might be because people tend to see them as other world creatures, worthy of stained glass windows. When we equate holiness with perfection, we then fail to notice all the truly holy people around us. They may never make the official list of the canonized but they could be of help to the preacher because they too have the good eye. They can see so much more than those with narrow, tunnel vision. The eyes of faith open up wide vistas: salvation, incarnation, resurrection. Karl Rahner says that "great Christianity and great poetry go together because the poet has radically faced who he or she is." Saints, like poets, keep pointing out the more to the preacher, the part of life some never notice.

Artists do another kind of modeling for preachers, best illustrated by painters and sculptors. Like the others, the good eye makes it possible for them to portray a bit of our world, a slice of our life. But even more often than the others, they must ask themselves what is appropriate. What bit of our world? Which slice of our life? The preacher asks himself the same questions.

Norman Rockwell is one of the best known of American artists. His work is familiar to most people because he did original covers for the popular *Saturday Evening Post* from 1916 to 1963. He may not be classified with the masters but he had a knack for putting the familiar on canvas. The down-home folks from Main Street America were his models, and they paraded past his easel for nearly three quarters of a century. Because his every work was well planned and fully detailed, he made countless decisions on the appropriate and inappropriate.

Rockwell did one cover for the *Post* in May of 1953 called "Outside the Principal's Office." It shows a disheveled little grammar school girl sitting on a bench sporting a black eye and a big grin. It is obvious that she has been in a fight, and the grin indicates that she has held her own, maybe even putting down the class bully. It is all there: scuffed shoes, rolled down socks, torn clothes, mussed hair and especially the grin. Over to the right, just barely included in the picture, you see the principal and a teacher peeking out the door of the office. Norman Rockwell spent hours deciding if the door to that office should be opened or closed. "What is appropriate?" he asked himself. He decided to leave the door open a bit so the principal and a concerned teacher could be seen. The homilist asks the same kind of questions of himself. What part of the message do I wish to give today? Am I including too much or not enough? Are there too many details? Am I wandering away from the central idea? Will this example help or distract? Like the artist, the homilist must be willing to invest time, think things out a little more, cross out, and begin again.

Cartoonists are another breed of artist who report meaningful life to us. They are not restricted to humor, but this would seem to be their chief concern. The good ones make us laugh but manage to also make us think. Sometimes a homily will do the same. In our day, Charles Schultz has become a favorite with preachers because so many lessons creep into his *Peanuts* strip. There is so much there: the arrogance of Lucy, the sad frown of Charlie Brown, the patience of Snoopy. These running cartoon stories can provide reference points known to preacher and to hearer. One of my favorites shows Charlie stretched out on the pitcher's mound, looking at the sky and musing: "I hate it when the baseball season is over. There's such a dreariness in the air that depresses me. Everything seems sad—even the old pitcher's mound is covered with weeds. I guess all a person can do is dream his dreams. Maybe I'll be a good ballplayer someday, maybe even play in the World Series and be a hero. I bet I will play in the World Series someday." Lucy then comes on the scene and shouts, "Hey, look who's out here talking to himself. What are you doing, Charlie Brown, thinking about all the times you struck out?" In the last box Charlie concludes: "There's a dreariness in the air that depresses me."

This could illustrate a variety of themes: self esteem, discouragement, the power of words, the virtue of charity and the like.

Although we have been concentrating on the artist, there are others who are not artists in the strict sense but do have a good eye. These are the people in our lives who slow us down to point out something along the way and say, "Will you look at that?"

A friend and I were driving through suburban New Jersey on a beautiful fall day. It was early morning and every half mile or so children were gathered in little clusters, waiting for the school bus. While they stood there in all shapes and sizes, they were doing the things children do when they stand in clusters: talking, laughing, shouting, pushing, thinking, daydreaming and playing their own special games. After I noticed only the color of the leaves, he pointed out to me the children. We both had the good eye but he saw more than I did. There are less obvious times too. Who hasn't noticed a child who sees something for the first time and had the feeling that the awe and wonder somehow rubbed off on you? One day I watched a two-year-old at a railroad station. I was merely taking a train, just one more bored commuter. The little girl was there on a special mission with her grandfather. They had come so that she could have a close look at a railroad train. The child looked, the grandfather looked, and because I was near them, when I looked, the train became something special for me too.

And, of course, there are the storytellers—people who not only have a knack for noticing but a great willingness to share with others what they notice. They are not only found sitting around a cracker barrel in a country store. We meet them in all kinds of places: cocktail parties, waiting on a line, tailgating before a football game, in the seat next to us on a plane, at a class reunion, even at a wake or funeral. (Should I say especially at a wake or funeral?) They seem to have a great zest for life, sharp powers of observation, and an uncanny ability for spotting the drama present in human encounters and life experiences. They have much to say to the preacher who is willing to listen to them.

This book brings together a group of people with a lot to say to the preacher. They are priest, bishop, mother, professional storyteller, woman religious, Scripture scholar, hospice counselor, editor, retreat director, seminary professor and even former clown. Some of them are artists in the strict sense of the word; more of them fall under the broader definition. They all have one thing in common: they are people with the good eye.

As for you, the reader—you too may have a good eye. Shout a loud hooray and be thankful. These chapters will affirm your approach, reconvince you and give you some new ideas as you sharpen your preaching skills. If you do not count a good eye among your blessings, this book will provide you with an opportunity to rub shoulders with people who do have the good eye.

Part I

Lights

A PREACHER'S NOTEBOOK—
PERSONAL RESOURCE CENTER

Robert F. Morneau

> Bishop Robert F. Morneau is auxiliary bishop in Green Bay, Wisconsin, the diocese where he was born and raised. Trained in philosophy and theology he taught both at Silver Lake College in Manitowoc, Wisconsin. He has published five books and a host of articles, mostly in the area of spiritual theology. In addition, Alba House has produced several of his lectures as cassettes. The bishop is in great demand as a speaker, and one of the secrets of his success is an ability to organize material and add a unique creative touch. For this reason we asked him to share with us some of his methodology.

A successful football coach in the area had the policy that his players must be systematically and frequently instructed regarding three things: *what* to do, *how* to do it, and *why* it should be done in this way. Success on the gridiron came with the imparting and exercise of these three things. Preaching raises the same three basic questions: what we are about in this important ministry, how we might become more effective preachers, and why we should be engaged in the proclaiming of God's word. This article is essentially pragmatic in that it deals with the "how-to" question. The tool suggested is a type of notebook in which the preacher stores a variety of reflections, observations and stories for future use. But before dealing with the pragmatic issue some brief reflections on the why and what of preaching are in order.

PREACHING: THE "WHY"

Nikos Kazantzakis has one of his characters cry out in *Zorba the Greek:* "Why! Why! Can't a man do anything without a why?" Perhaps it is possible to do something for a short period of time without asking the meaning question but eventually it must be addressed. The ultimate *why* of preaching is to reveal the living and true God so that people can respond to his presence and power. Preaching is an invitation to the fullness of life that comes to us in Jesus. Preaching sounds a trumpet to awaken us to conversion and the joy of salvation. Preaching reminds us of who we are and where we are going. What a noble, privileged ministry!

PREACHING: THE "WHAT"

The mission and ministry of Jesus has been given to the Church. This involves proclaiming the Kingdom of God and translating that proclamation into action. All Christians in some way are called to this task. In a unique manner the preaching function fulfills this twofold ministry. The preacher is to provide a vision of the Kingdom that will help people know what they are about in following the Lord; the preacher is to stir people to action so that the heart is touched and the deed, the Gospel deed, is accomplished.

Perhaps one reason for the popularity of *National Geographic* is that almost every issue contains some type of map giving the reader a new perspective of some part of the world. Preaching provides an overview by which people can interpret their everyday life in the light of God's word. Meaning comes when we make connections. By connecting liturgy and life the preacher helps people to see—an essential part of the preaching task. Vision is no small grace.

As our minds demand clarity, so our hearts need values to call us to conversion. Often the Bible challenges us to allow our stony hearts to become hearts of flesh. Preaching fosters large-heartedness in proclaiming Gospel values: love, forgiveness, compassion, humility, gentleness. Reaching beyond the mind to the deep recesses of the heart, preaching enkindles our affectivity with the power and presence of God. The dynamic and emotive function of preaching relates directly to the process of helping people internalize values that will shape their judgments and actions. Often these values are transmitted by means of stories, images and symbols that clarify, integrate and motivate our inner lives.

No ministry, be it parenting, teaching or preaching, would be complete without in some way involving behavior. Both individual life-style and collective activity become the object of preaching. We call people to virtue: "To act justly, to love tenderly, to walk humbly with our God." Homilies are more than mere invitations. They contain an imperative that demands a response. Without being "preachy" we are to challenge and confront any behavior that is not congruent with the life of Jesus and with his mission.

PREACHING: "THE HOW-TO"

In accomplishing the preaching ministry one tool is to keep a notebook in which one can file, in appropriate sections, materials that will help to explain and elucidate the word of God. Each preacher will have a different approach to life, but basically the notebook saver would be on the lookout for three types of experiences—experiences that help us to see, that stir our hearts, that call us to action. My own personal notebook for preaching contains three sections: I: VISION; II: VALUES; III: VIRTUES. The vision section records overviews, statements and insights that provide meaning for the journey. The value section notes stories, cartoons and images that have an affective component. The virtue section lists life situations in which people act out what they can see and feel providing an example of a positive or negative nature. Sample entries in each section will be given as one possible approach to developing a preacher's notebook.

Section I: Vision

"Nothing in nature is isolated; nothing is without reference to something else; nothing achieves meaning apart from that which neighbors it." So says Goethe. With this realization the preacher's notebook searches for quotations, perspectives and insights that help both the preacher and those he ministers to, to see the breadth and depth of reality. A key to effective preaching (and all teaching, for that matter) is to contextualize: to put what we are speaking about into a frame of reference which allows for meaning. For example, in preaching about peace we must see the relationship between peace and four other qualities: truth, justice, freedom and charity (John XXIII); in preaching about redemption we must position this doctrine in reference to sin; in speaking about the Church we must know who Jesus is and how the plan of God the Father was fulfilled through him. Things spoken of outside their frame of reference lack meaning. The vision section of a preacher's notebook fosters large perspectives within which we situate various elements of our faith life.

Here are four examples from my own notebook which help me to preach contextually. The first is a quotation from Pope John XXIII's *Pacem in Terris* (#167) that provides a vision of peace. I then drew two planetary systems showing what the demands of peace are and what are the contrasting realities:

Sec. I: Vision p. 14   **Topic: PEACE**

Source: John XXIII's *Pacem in Terris*, #167.

"However, peace will be but an empty-sounding word unless it is founded on the order which this present document has outlined in confident hope: an order founded on truth, built according to justice, vivified and integrated by charity, and put into practice in freedom."

Diagrams:

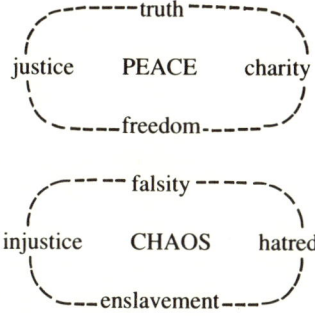

Another entry in the vision section of my notebook deals with the concept and the context of ministry. The word "ministry" is used in many senses today. This entry shows ministry as the top of an iceberg and is related to four other large concepts that lie beyond the water line. Ministry, which deals with people who use their gifts in meeting the needs of others, is grounded in mission. Mission can only be understood in the context of Church, and obviously our notion of Church is rooted in our notion of Jesus and God. Thus the entry pictorially links these various faith realities together with the iceberg as the working metaphor:

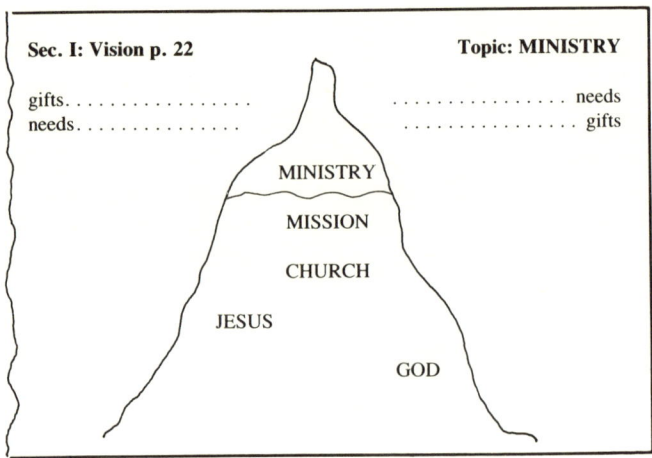

A third example of the vision section deals with the important topic of formation of conscience. The entry attempts to deal with the question of what are the major ingredients in the making of a moral, Christian decision. The baseball diamond demonstrates that a decision should touch all four bases if it is to be complete and mature: the decision should come from the person (internalized), it should be respectful of the rights and dignity of others, it should be based on solid information and it should be in accord with the Gospel and the teaching of the Church. The entry attempts to capture this important process:

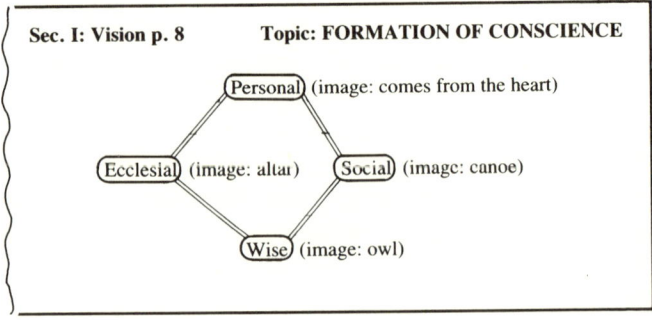

A central concern in the Church has always been spirituality. Another entry in my notebook notes the major components in the spiritual life: spirituality involves a threefold relationship. Through prayer we deepen our relationship with God; through asceticism (mortification, discipline) we gain an interior freedom in relationship to ourselves; through service we reach out into the lives of our brothers and sisters. The triangle symbolizes the interdependence among these spiritual activities of prayer (P), asceticism (A), and service (S):

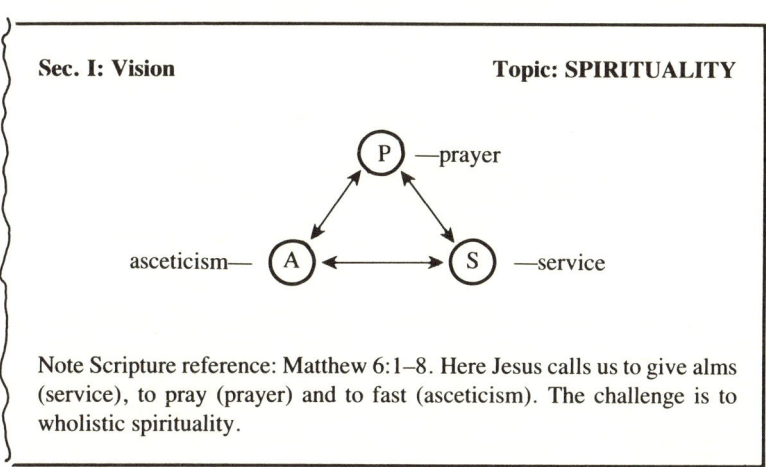

Sec. I: Vision   **Topic: SPIRITUALITY**

Note Scripture reference: Matthew 6:1–8. Here Jesus calls us to give alms (service), to pray (prayer) and to fast (asceticism). The challenge is to wholistic spirituality.

Section II: Values

Values are the source of action. This section of the notebook, used to make our preaching more effective and meaningful, deals with stories, images and symbols that help to stir the heart. Storytelling drives home a principle or insight; humorous anecdotes are remembered far longer than abstract ideas; images and symbols energize an inert heart. The homily reaches beyond the mind and attempts to enlarge our affective life. The notebook records possible examples that might be used in making our homilies effective.

Stories, those from fiction and real life, catch our fancy. The "once upon a time" hooks the child within us and can be an effective instrument of illustrating some Gospel value. An example from the notebook:

> **Sec. II: Values (stories) p. 11   Topic: IT'S WHOM YOU KNOW!**
> A good friend of mine was telling of her son's recent experience on the ski hill. Coming off the chair lift, he was accosted by two Jehovah's Witnesses with the question: "Are you saved?" The fifteen year old was not to be intimidated. His short, quick response was: "Sure, I'm saved!" Surprised if not irritated the Jehovah's Witnesses challenged: "How do you know you're saved?" Again the quick retort: "Because my mom knows two priests and the bishop!"

Quotations and aphorisms can be very substantial. In just a sentence or a few words, a meaningful truth can be presented in a form that is easily remembered. The preacher's notebook should always be at hand to make new entries:

> **Sec. II: Values (quotations) p. 6** **Topic: VALUES**
>
> ". . . essential values become clear only through practice."
> (Romano Guardini's *The Lord*)
>
> "Learn what to take seriously and laugh at the rest."
> (Herman Hesse's *Steppenwolf*)
>
> "We have bartered holiness for convenience, loyalty for success, love for power, wisdom for information, tradition for fashion."
> (Abraham Heschel's *Man's Quest for God*)
>
> "Moral values make us what we are as persons. Moral values make us human. Failure here is drastic, not just unfortunate."
> (Daniel Maguire's *The Moral Choice*)
>
> "The multiplicity of the world will crowd in on me again with its false sense of values. Values weighed in quantity, not quality; in speed, not stillness; in noise, not silence; in words, not in thoughts; in acquisitiveness, not beauty. How shall I resist the onslaught?"
> (Anne Morrow Lindbergh's *Gift from the Sea*)

One way to concretize our values is through symbols and images. In his popular and helpful book *Models of the Church,* Fr. Avery Dulles writes: "Symbols transform the horizons of man's life, integrate his perception of reality, alter his scale of values, reorient his loyalties, attachments and aspirations in a manner far exceeding the powers of abstract conceptual thought" (p. 24). Given this fact, a preacher should keep his eye out for images and symbols that serve the above functions (transforming, integrating, altering) in human life. An area of the notebook could be used to record symbols, images and metaphors that help to interpret, broaden and deepen experience:

Sec. II: Values p. 32   **Topic: IMAGES**

I saw

   . . . the melodic geese southward bound,
       and a September desire seeking a more mild climate.

   . . . the dead balloon lying in the July ditch
       and searched the landscape for a saddened child.

   . . . the splendid yellow of jubilant daisies,
       and wondered if God's paint brush was yet dry.

   . . . the fragile, submissive eyes of a lonely soul,
       and questioned how much weight the human heart can bear.

   . . . the caterpillar inch its way across a country road
       and thought of our planet inching its way through a vast universe.

I heard

   . . . the August crickets all speaking together at their annual convention
       and guessed at the winter policies being formed.

   . . . the key enter the lock and do its work
       and saw loving words bring freedom to the captivated heart.

   . . . the weak thunder of a distant, speeding jet
       and there arose a whither, a whence and a why.

   . . . in the darkness of the night the sound of the mosquito on its bombing raids and sank more deeply under the covers to avoid detection.

   . . . behind me a morning yawn coming from the land of Orpheus and found it impossible not to respond with my own.

Section III: Virtues

Jesus called people to action—to do the truth in love. Accurate doctrine and deep, sincere sentiment is not sufficient for Christian living. The proof is in the pudding, in the doing. The notebook records excerpts from movies which depict people in their fragile relationships and struggles. Biographies are a gold mine in providing examples of actual lives. Sometimes the modeling is exemplary, at other times the very antithesis of Christian love. Novels and short stories also are invaluable sources for vicariously experiencing a wide range of human values. A well-read preacher is an interesting preacher.

The methodology of recording entries varies here according to the material. What is important is to provide a context so that those who have not seen the movie, read the book or been entertained by the play will be able to understand what is taking place. Also, because of faulty memory, the notebook helps the preacher to recall with some accuracy the scene from the various sources. Here are some examples from my own collection:

Sec. III: Virtues (movies) p. 14   **Topic: LOVE**

E.T. One of the last scenes in the movie depicts little E.T., the dear friend of the earthling Eliot, about to die. All of modern technology with the latest sophisticated equipment is unable to keep E.T.'s heart going. With tears in his eyes, Eliot bends over E.T. and says: "I love you." At once the heart begins to beat and life re-enters his friend.

Sec. III: Virtues (play) p. 4   **Topic: CONSCIENCE**

A Man for All Seasons
Sir Thomas More, the chancellor of England under Henry VIII, was being coerced into making a decision which he knew was not right. His courage and strength withstood the coercion and he held to his own conviction. A powerful line from Robert Bolt's play says it well: "And when we stand before God, and you are sent to Paradise for doing according to your conscience, and I am damned for not doing according to mine, will you come with me, for fellowship?"

In her excellent novel *To Kill a Mockingbird,* Harper Lee provides her audience with a sensitive account of two small children growing up in the South amidst injustice and hatred. The lawyer father of the two children, Atticus Finch, tells the children of a certain quality he saw in an elderly lady the children had to attend to in her last illness, an illness which made her far from pleasant. The notebook contains a quotation regarding courage:

Sec. III: Virtues (novel) p. 9   Topic: COURAGE

"I wanted you to see something about her—I wanted you to see what real courage is, instead of getting the idea that courage is a man with a gun in his hand. It's when you know you're licked before you begin but you begin anyway and you see it through no matter what. You rarely win, but sometimes you do. Mrs. Dubose won, all ninety-eight pounds of her. According to her views, she died beholden to nothing and nobody. She was the bravest person I ever knew."
(Harper Lee's *To Kill a Mockingbird,* New York: Fawcett Popular Library, 1960, p. 116)

Sec. III: Virtues (quotations)   Topic: VIRTUE

"The ancients called beauty the flowering of virtue."
(Ralph Waldo Emerson)

"Nothing is more unpleasant than a virtuous person with a mean mind."
(Walter Bagehot)

"An act of virtue produces in a man mildness, peace, comfort, light, purity, and strength, just as inordinate appetite brings about torment, fatigue, weariness, blindness and weakness."
(John of the Cross)

"For all the vices are seasoned with pride just as the virtues are seasoned and enlivened by charity."
(Catherine of Siena)

"God is present, Christ is present, wherever there is enacted between one man and another an act of supernatural virtue."
(Simone Weil)

"Pride is the downward drag of all things into an easy solemnity. One 'settles down' into a sort of selfish seriousness; but one has to rise to a gay self-forgetfulness. A man 'falls' into a brown study; he reaches up at a blue sky. Seriousness is not a virtue."
(G.K. Chesterton)

Technology deals with the translating of vision into reality. It means having the equipment and tools to facilitate the process. Keeping a personal notebook can be one instrument that enriches our proclaiming the word of God. Its main advantages are to provide abundant examples, to concretize our ideas through images and stories, and to make the word of God more alive to the people. Over a period of years the notebook grows fat in its accumulated wealth, at least from external observation; it remains slim within because of frequent and effective use.

THOUGHTS ON STORYTELLING

Jay O'Callaghan

> Jay O'Callaghan calls himself a story maker who creates his own tales. *Time* calls him a "genius among the storytellers" and a "man of poetry and elegance." He lives in Marshfield, Mass. but performs his special kind of theater all over the world and manages to find time to make records and movies. We wondered what a professional of his caliber would say to the preacher. He is truly a person in the pew and indeed a talented one with much to offer.

The human voice has probably been used for ten thousand years, perhaps far longer. But before humans discovered voice they probably danced a story, or drew a story in a cave. The drawing might show a stick figure standing then lying down. The first story of death.

Elizabeth Coatsworth, the poet and writer, once wrote to me saying, "From the first people probably gathered around a fire to explore life through stories; they explored the conscious and unconscious, the frightening and the ordinary." Stories are a way of exploring life.

A need for stories seems to be imprinted on the human psyche—and for good reason. We each live our story and we're all part of the larger story of cultures, nations and the story of the human race. We are all part of the final story of the sun, the universe, the creation.

In listening to stories and telling them we remind ourselves of the richness and complexity of our own stories. Stories dignify us. They remind us we are important. Freud discovered that listening to someone's story was important. The teller realized what he or she was saying was important and freeing and healing. In prayer, we tell our story to Christ. In the sacrament of reconciliation, we share our story with the confessor and together celebrate the good news that Christ loves us and our story—even or maybe especially the painful part.

The hunger for stories today is extraordinary. The stories are largely told in movies, television programs, novels, theater and opera, but the purest form of story is the told story. All that's needed is the teller and the tale.

The best storyteller I ever heard in church was Father Joseph McFarlane, S.J. When I first saw Father McFarlane at St. Christine's Church in Marshfield, Massachusetts, he looked so old and slow I expected a feeble sermon. Father McFarlane began, and soon I was laughing and full of wonder, for he was taking us on a journey to Rome and Greece, then to the 1930's in Brooklyn. I forgot his age and his infirmities. I was on a journey with a wonderful man. And that journey helped bring me back to the Church. Father McFarlane's stories were lit with compassion, with humor, with a love for people and life.

Father Joseph McFarlane, S.J. studied Oriental theology in Rome before World War II. The war disrupted his schooling plans and he returned to the United States to edit Jesuit publications. When he retired, Father McFarlane assisted at St. Christine's Parish in Marshfield. St. Christine's parishioners listened to his story sermons and saw that he was a wise wonderful man.

One Christmas Eve Father Joe McFarlane said he was always amazed that the Creator had chosen the host as a way to be present to us. The storyteller is always aware of the image. Perhaps the most stunning image of our existence is the image of the host being raised and becoming the body and blood of Christ. A storyteller makes us aware afresh of what is before us. The storyteller can make us resee the beauty of that simple wafer—divine bread.

The ability to tell stories comes with practice. And with thought. And observation. Jesus was a storyteller. He observed life around him—grapevines, vineyards, laborers, Samaritans, weddings. And Jesus wove all the details of life about him into the fundamental form of teaching story, the parable. Times have changed since Jesus' time but the hunger for stories hasn't changed. I suggest you look at the details of your life and of life about you and weave your memories and observations into stories.

Storytelling is a different form and requires some exploring. Storytelling is an oral form, a form of sound and imagery woven into a narrative. Sermons are often impersonal in that they are reasoned messages which enlighten and give us pause to reflect on our actions. Storytelling is very personal and can achieve the same ends. As you tell a story you give a sense of who you are. Your sense of humor, hope, wit, intensity are all revealed. People appreciate and are moved by what is most human in us. The very process of telling a story seems to draw forth what's best in us.

In Halifax, Nova Scotia one August Sunday a Nigerian priest said the Mass. His sermon was well thought out and carefully delivered. It revealed little, however, of the man. After the last prayer the Nigerian priest stepped forward and said a few words about his boyhood in Nigeria. He told brief stories of his youth. Suddenly we all saw *him* and were so charmed and warmed that we burst into applause.

As a storyteller I think it is wonderful that Christ chose stories as his medium, for he must have revealed himself in every telling. Doubtless he warmed and charmed and challenged the hearts of his hearers.

I often wonder why readers never change their voices when Moses is speaking, or St. Paul, or Peter, or Jesus. Embarrassment, I suppose. It seems a hidden commandment that the Gospel must be read in a monotone. That's the print voice, not the human voice of everyday. The voice is a musical instrument. It varies with emotion and conviction and with each person. Let's hear that variety when the Gospel is read. Let's hear the excitement when the prodigal son returns, let's feel the bitterness of the faithful son and let's feel the compassion in the father's voice.

SUGGESTIONS ON TELLING STORIES

1. Try out a short story. Sit down and tell it alone—a story of 1–3 minutes. Then explore it. What makes it come alive? A character? An image? A sense of sadness or lightness? What are the verbs that make it sing? Is there any baggage that can be cut? By telling a story to yourself and keeping a time limit, you may force the clearest language, the clearest image, the most succinct dialogue. I've recorded some stories for Dial A Story in New York City and am fascinated by the forty-second story. One of the great storytellers of our time, Ken Feit, wanted to compress the Iliad to a minute. Ken knew the beauty of compression. Compression isn't always the answer, but with preachers I'd suggest it's a good place to start.

Once, in the land of the Walnut there was a preacher who loved people. He wanted to encourage them, for he knew life was a struggle. His sermons were good but long. One week he had no ideas. The week moved along and he had no ideas. He was desperate. Sunday he stepped into the pulpit and looked at all those faces. He turned red and blurted, "Yesssssssssssssssssssss!" And left. Best sermon he ever gave.

2. Examine the image in the story; perhaps it will illuminate your sermon. Images condense reality. In the parable of the prodigal son the image of the father looking up and seeing his wayward son returning is a joyful stilling image. It lights the moment up. He's glad! An image is concrete; it's visual. The listeners hear the words and make the image. Each sees the moment of the son returning differently. A father who is unreconciled with his one son may see two images at once.

3. Explore sound. Discover your strengths. You may be very good at being quiet or you may be too quiet or too fast.

Use repetition or rhythm if either seems appropriate. Gioia Timpanelli of New York is a masterful storyteller and uses question in the middle of the story in a startling way. "Who is that man?" Gioia will suddenly say. "Who is that man?" In the middle of the story Gioia makes us stop and wonder.

Life is full of rhythm and sounds. You may want to make the sound of the wind or the sound of a bell or of someone knocking.

4. If you use gestures, make them tell. A gesture can be extremely dramatic and yet so much in keeping with the tale that it just seems natural. What you want is to discover your own way of telling a story. Storytelling is a very personal matter. My style is highly dramatic; I take the part of every character and use motion and song. That is one way. A student of mine at the Lesley Graduate School told a story at the end of the course that was stunning. The student, a Japanese woman, dressed in white, told the story of a swan. She was perfectly still as she told it, until the swan moved, and at that moment the teller lifted her arm in a simple but breathtaking gesture.

Make your gestures tell.

5. Be aware of place in a story. Be aware of dust and heat, and the smells and tastes and voices of a place. Christ walked a lot; somehow that's comforting. He lived in heat and knew the beauty of shade. He knew the taste of wine, the smell of sweat, oil, fish, dates, donkeys, and camels. If we have some sense of the place he lived in, we get a better sense of his humanity.

The imagination likes to know where it is, so be aware of where the story is taking place. All humans live in some place, and it's up to the teller to give the listeners a sense of place.

A person's place is his theater. As a boy, St. Mary's Rectory in Brookline, Massachusetts was a place, a theater of mystery to me. What did the priests do in there? Did they sit at the table and laugh over meals? Were they very quiet? Was all a hush? We're all curious about the place where others live. Knowing this might stimulate you to tell some stories about places that are important to you.

Be aware of the place you tell your story. If it is a church, be aware of the sacred theater you are speaking in. If there are candles burning on the altar, let them calm you and realize that as fire is elemental, so are stories. The Mass itself is extraordinarily elemental. Fire and water, wine and bread, the sacred vestments, the mixing of water and wine, the lifting of the chalice and the host, the sacred prayers. What better place for stories—the elemental form of drama!

6. Be gentle with yourself. Compliment yourself on telling a story. Give it as a gift, then let it go. Stories require an openness. They are an invitation to go on a journey that only works if the listeners are willing to trust you as a guide. Thus you're vulnerable when telling. If people listen, wonderful; if they don't, it's awful. But while most stories work, there are failures. I once told a favorite story at a formal dinner for substitute teachers at a country club. It was a long story about a grasshopper, tested before perhaps two hundred audiences; now my listeners grew stiff and very silent. They had turned to stone. Stone does not giggle or applaud. When I finished they returned to life, and I fled. An awful time, but there was a bright spot. I had the power to turn them to stone. Storytelling demands that you take a chance; there are times when it won't work. But usually it will reach where ordinary sermons never can.

There is a need for vision and dreams. That's why story is important. It lets us touch the wonder, passion and mystery of life. And it lets us gather around language, the teller and the tale. Hearing a story often gives us a glimpse of the beauty and the sacredness of life and of our own story.

When I tell a story and it really works I sense a powerful mood of acceptance—a letting go of narrownesss, of worries, of restriction and an acceptance in the largest sense, an acceptance of the story, of the world of the story and an acceptance of life. There is a sense of accepting the wonder of sacredness of being human. What a wonderful reward that feeling is.

THE LECTIONARY: TOO MUCH OF A GOOD THING?

William Skudlarek, O.S.B.

> Rev. William Skudlarek, a Benedictine, is the dean/rector of the School of Theology at St. John's, Collegeville, Minnesota. His doctorate is from Princeton Theological Seminary where he specialized in preaching. He is one of the principal authors of *Fulfilled in Your Hearing: The Homily in the Sunday Assembly,* a well-received publication of the N.C.C.B. Because of his writing and lecturing, he is fast becoming a prime mover in the current efforts to improve the quality of preaching. We asked him to answer a common question: How can you use Scripture without making of your homily an exegetical exercise?

> The treasures of the Bible should be opened up more lavishly so that richer fare might be provided for the faithful at the table of God's word (Vatican II, Constitution on the Sacred Liturgy, #51).

The scriptural fare which the lectionary provides for the liturgical assembly and for its preachers is almost too rich. Week after week preachers turn to the Scriptures for the coming Sunday and wonder how they can possibly do justice to an Old Testament lesson, a psalm, a New Testament lesson, and a Gospel in a homily that will normally last less than a quarter of an hour.

Certainly a homily should do justice to the Scriptures, interpreting them accurately and presenting this interpretation clearly and cogently. But accurate exegesis and clear teaching are not the primary purpose of the homily. They are means to an end. The homily's *raison d'être* is, rather, to do justice to the assembly which has gathered for worship by leading it to deeper faith and to the expression of that faith in worship and in life. If the purpose of the lectionary is "primarily a pastoral one, in the spirit of the

Second Vatican Council,"[1] then the purpose of the preaching which flows from that lectionary is also pastoral. It responds to people's actual needs and experiences, speaks a language and draws on images with which they are familiar, and enables them to see their lives as a gift of God for which they can praise him and with which they can serve him.

We might continue the gastronomic analogy used by the Constitution on the Sacred Liturgy and describe the lectionary as more a buffet than a banquet. The preacher functions in the role of a host preparing a plate for a guest. The objective is not so much to take a little of everything but to choose what the guest likes and needs: no sweets for the diabetic, lots of raw vegetables for the person who wants to lose weight. In a similar way, the preacher at the table of the lectionary needs to exercise choice, choice based on a pastoral sensitivity to the needs and abilities of the particular congregation for whom the homily will be prepared and preached.

SUNDAYS THROUGH THE YEAR

How, in practice, can a homilist use the lectionary in order to preach pastorally? During the Sundays in Ordinary Time it is proper to look first of all to the Gospel as the principal source for the homily.[2] Liturgical tradition has, from its earliest times, accorded primacy to the reading of the Gospel in the liturgy of the word. It is proclaimed by an ordained minister, surrounded with signs of honor and reverence, and placed last in the order of readings. The Gospel lesson is also the controlling lesson for the lit-

---

1. Introduction to the Lectionary, chapter 2, section IX. In the Liturgical Press edition of the lectionary (Collegeville, Minn.: 1970), p. xxxii.
2. I refer to the Gospel as the principal *scriptural* source of the homily because a homily always has two sources: the Scriptures and human experience.

urgy of the word in Ordinary Time. Each of the Synoptic Gospels is read through over a three-year cycle, and it is in light of each Gospel pericope that the Old Testament lesson and responsorial psalm have been chosen. The prestigious position of the Gospel in the liturgy, as well as the relative familiarity and accessibility of the Gospel passages, predisposes and prepares a congregation for preaching which is more closely related to it than to the other scriptural lessons.

Although the Gospel will normally be the principal scriptural source for the homily, the preacher should continue to read and, as far as time allows, give time to the exegesis of the other scriptural texts of the liturgy of the word. This reading and study need not be done with any express intention of referring to all three readings and the psalm in the homily. Such tying together of all the readings may constitute a homiletical *tour de force,* but rarely makes the homily more effective as the word of God. The purpose of continuing to read the other texts is rather to allow these texts to establish a hermeneutical dialogue among themselves. The dialogue which will take place between the Gospel and the Old Testament texts—first reading and psalm—is fairly predictable, given the fact that the Old Testament reading was chosen to harmonize with the Gospel and thus to show "the basic unity of both Testaments and of the history of salvation: a unity which has Christ in the memorial of his paschal mystery as its center."[3] One may argue that this is too restrictive an approach to the Old Testament, but it is the principle by which the texts of the Old Testament have been selected for the Sundays in Ordinary Time. A fuller, richer reading of the Old Testament at the Sunday Eucharist will have to await a future revision of the current lectionary.

The second reading in Ordinary Time, however, has no intrinsic relation to the Gospel pericope, and for that very reason the dialogue between it and the Gospel can be much more creative.

---

3. Introduction to the Lectionary, chapter 1, section IIa (p. xxvii).

When referring to the presence of difficult scriptural texts in the lectionary, the Introduction states, "Frequently a passage will become easier to grasp when associated with another reading from the same Mass."[4] In a similar way the conjunction of two completely unrelated readings can alert the preacher to a level of meaning, a *sensus plenior,* if you will, that might otherwise never be noticed.

The meaning which emerges from the dialogue of texts can never be forced, and if none comes forth, well and good. But on the other hand, the homilist should not simply ignore the second reading on the grounds that it is not thematically related to the Gospel, as is the Old Testament lesson. The very fact that it is unrelated is what makes the textual dialogue such a powerful source for creative insight, for "creativity occurs when two ideas seemingly unrelated to each other come together in such a way that they create something new, an original pattern of things."[5]

But back to the Gospel which remains the principal text of the liturgy of the word and the text to which the homilist will devote the most time and effort in preparing the homily. As the preacher reads, prays over, and studies the text of the Gospel (all three approaches to the text are essential), it is important that the right questions be asked of it. If the preacher approaches the text simply as an ancient document and asks what it meant in its original historical context, it will be possible to give an informative, even interesting lecture on it. But that is not yet preaching. Or, if the preacher approaches the text looking for helpful lessons on the way we are to live our lives (or, as is unfortunately more often the case, on the way the people are to live *their* lives), the homily will almost always be little more than a moralistic exhortation to do

---

4. *Ibid.,* chapter 1, section VIc (p. xxix).
5. Bill Moyers, "Defining Creativity for Everyone Wasn't Exactly Easy," *Smithsonian* (January 1982), p. 72.

better, with lots of musts and shoulds, but with very little of the Gospel vision which makes Gospel living possible. The homily will offer plenty of good advice, but very little of the good news that enables people to put the good advice into practice.

But if the homilist approaches the text of the Gospel asking, "What is the human situation behind this text? Why was this word spoken or written in the first place? Why was it remembered? To what continuing need in the life of the Church did it provide a word from the Lord? How was it heard as good news by those early followers of Jesus? How can it be heard as good news today? By the congregation to whom I will preach? By me?" If the homilist can interact with the text with questions like these, the homily that will emerge is much more likely to be an expression of the good news of God's continuing love for his people (a love which is not without its challenges and demands) and will therefore all the more easily serve to lead the congregation to worship this God with praise and thanksgiving in the liturgy of the Eucharist.

Prayerful dialogue with the text, done either by oneself or in a group, needs to be supplemented by serious exegetical study. As important as it is to let the text speak to us immediately, we cannot ignore the fact that biblical texts emerged in a world and a culture far different from ours. Furthermore, the Bible is not our private possession. It is the faith document of a Church community which has a tradition of interpreting individual texts in the light of its overarching understanding of the whole word of God. The homilist, therefore, cannot be content with "what the text says to me." In addition to a pastoral concern for the needs of the community, the homilist will also be concerned to do justice to the Scriptures by studying them with the aid of the best exegetical tools available: commentaries, dictionaries, concordances, Gospel parallels, and the like.

A week of reflection, prayer, and study of the Sunday Gospel, plus continued reading and reflection on the other lessons of the liturgy of the word, will provide the preacher with more than enough material for the Sunday homily. Once again, a choice will have to be made. Of the many possibilities for a homily, which will be of most benefit to this particular congregation at this particular time? Having made that choice, always a difficult one because of the many good ideas and images that will have to be let go for another time, the preacher then needs to determine how to present this idea or image in a way that will make for effective communication with the congregation. Some helpful strategies for the organization and communication of the homily can be found in the other chapters of this book.

ADVENT, LENT, AND EASTER

Preaching from the Gospel during the Sundays in Ordinary Time is not an absolute rule, by any means. There may be times when a particular pastoral concern may more easily be addressed from another scriptural text, or from one or the other prayers of the liturgy, for that matter. It may also be appropriate at times to preach a series of homilies on the *lectio continua* of the second reading. What is inappropriate, however, is jumping from one text to another on successive Sundays for no other reason than the personal whim of the preacher.

During the major liturgical seasons of the year, however, as well as on feast days, the Gospel does not function as the controlling lesson on the lectionary in the same way as it does in Ordinary Time. On these Sundays and feastdays, therefore, it may make more sense—again, in the light of pastoral realities—to relate the homily more closely to a scriptural text other than the Gospel.

For example, during Lent the Old Testament readings are chosen to present the development of salvation history, "one of the main topics of Lenten instruction,"⁶ rather than because of any link to the Gospel. During the Easter season the first lesson is from the Acts of the Apostles, and texts are chosen which present the "life, growth, and witness of the early Church."⁷ Over the three year cycle the second lesson during the Easter season is chosen from 1 Peter, 1 John, and the Book of Revelation. These texts are "appropriate to the spirit of the Easter season, a spirit of joyful faith and confident hope."⁸ During Advent the readings from Isaiah and Paul are also chosen because of their relation to the liturgical season, rather than to the text of the Gospel, and can therefore provide the immediate scriptural basis for a series of seasonal homilies. In all these cases it is the Gospel which can now be read alongside the other texts and brought into dialogue with them.

SPECIAL OCCASIONS

Under the headings "Ritual Masses" and "Masses for Various Occasions" the lectionary provides scriptural texts for the celebration of the sacraments, for funerals and blessings, and also for Masses celebrated for specific groups (e.g., pastoral or spiritual meetings), times (e.g., in time of war or civil disturbance), or needs (e.g., for productive land). The choice of texts for a particular celebration is to be determined by "the particular occasion and the pastoral needs of the participating group."⁹ Preachers are well advised to consult the complete lectionary in making such choices, and not to rely on booklets which are provided for wedding or funeral services. Often these booklets contain only a

---

6. Introduction to the Lectionary, chapter 2, section II (p. xxxiv).
7. *Ibid.*, chapter 2, section IV (p. xxxiv).
8. *Ibid.* (p. xxxv).
9. *Ibid.*, chapter 1, section V (p. xxviii).

handful of the options given in the lectionary and thus severely limit the "rich fare . . . of God's word" which the lectionary provides.

An appropriate choice of Scripture lessons will depend, in large measure, on how well the preacher knows the individuals involved or the congregation that gathers for the particular occasion. When personal knowledge is lacking, as would be the case, for example, in the sudden death of a parishioner who was not well known, it becomes especially important to find ways to involve family and friends in the choice of appropriate texts. By inviting such involvement the preacher will be better able to hear and to speak the word which God speaks to his people, revealing the mystery of their redemption and salvation and offering them spiritual nourishment.[10]

---

10. See General Instruction of the Roman Missal, #33. In the Liturgical Press edition of the Sacramentary (Collegeville, Minn.: 1974), p. 24.

USING LITERATURE
James C. Turro

> Rev. James C. Turro is a biblical scholar, author, lecturer and retreat master. After a short time as an associate in a parish, he attended the Biblical Institute in Rome, where he received an S.S.L. Since then, he has been professor of Sacred Scripture at the Darlington Seminary, Archdiocese of Newark and teaches in several other seminaries and universities. His special gifts make him just as comfortable in pastoral ministry as he is in the academic world. He has been weekend associate in the same parish for thirty-odd years and has developed an appealing preaching style. We asked him to reflect on the use of literature in the homily.

Someone has drawn an arresting distinction between exegesis and preaching: exegesis takes the student by the hand and leads him into the world of the biblical text, whereas preaching moves in the opposite direction—it takes a teaching and seeks to bring it home to the hearer.[1] It is my conviction that the use of literature is of immeasurable value in doing just that—bringing a given truth of faith into the consciousness of the hearer with clarity and grace.

I could begin by suggesting that there is a certain kinship between literature and Christian preaching. For one thing, literature and preaching, each in its own way, often deal with the same subjects. I am reminded of a comment made about Muriel Spark's books: "All of Muriel Spark's novels are in one way or another, sly, frequently droll meditations on the Four Last Things—which is another way of saying they are about good and evil, God and the Devil."[2] I believe this remark can with justice be enlarged to

---

1. This distinction was first proposed, as far as I can tell, by Gerhard von Rad, *Predigt-Meditationen,* Vandenhoeck & Ruprecht (Göttingen, 1973) p. 15. The distinction recommended itself to von Rad upon his reading an observation about translation made by F. Schleiermacher, *Sämtliche Werke,* III, 2, pp. 207ff.

2. Barbara Grizzuti Harrison, *New York Times Book Review,* Sunday, March 31, 1981 (review of Muriel Spark's *Loitering with Intent*).

cover not just Miss Spark's work but much of world literature. This same notion was more peremptorily expressed by Raissa Maritain: "Only theology and poetry can speak of God, knowledge, inspiration and experience."[3] Literature though it recounts the stories of individual human beings is really speaking to us of the common human experience. Rollo May has justly remarked: "Aeschylus' Orestes and Goethe's Faust, to take two diverse examples, are not simply portrayals of two given characters, one back in Greece in the fifth century B.C. and the other in eighteenth century Germany, but presentations of the struggles we all, of whatever century or race, go through in growing up, trying to find identity as individual beings, striving to affirm our being with whatever power we have, trying to love and create and doing our best to meet all the other events of life up to and including our own death."[4] Robert Alter has put it still more concisely: "We learn through fiction because we encounter in it the translucent images the writer has cunningly projected out of an intuitively grasped fund of experience not dissimilar to our own, only shaped, defined, ordered, probed in ways we never manage in the muddled and diffuse transactions of our lives."[5] One can judge from the above to what a remarkable degree literature covers the same ground as Christian preaching does. To recapitulate: literature and preaching have at least this much in common: they both treat of the deep realities of life and eternity. There is of course another fairly obvious resemblance between preaching and literature in that they both proceed toward their goal in a similar fashion. They seek to speak their piece with greater snap and

---
3. *Raissa's Journal*, presented by Jacques Maritain, Magi Books (Albany, N.Y., 1963), p. 328.
4. Rollo May, *Love and Will*, Dell (New York, 1969), p. 20.
5. Robert Alter, *The Art of Biblical Narrative*, Basic Books (New York, 1981), p. 156.

pungency and with greater depth as well than is done, say, in ordinary conversation.[6]

How is one to take advantage of what literature has to give? The sobering fact is that literature does not yield up its wealth to the preacher upon demand. One who goes looking to literature for an episode, a line, a phrase that will shore up the idea he is developing, could conceivably read through miles of text, for days on end and still not be rewarded with what he needs.

There is an obvious short-cut that will suggest itself here—the use of collections of quotations. This could be the handiest, most direct access to the riches that literature has to offer—a gleaning of cogent and striking passages, all conveniently indexed by topic. My own experience has been that the quotations presented in sumptuous array at times prove to be time-worn and border on cliché. At other times the only merit a quotation appears to have is to have been written by a renowned author, but of itself it conveys no dazzling insight and makes no enlightening comment. Manifestly, this tool, the book of quotations, must be used judiciously.

Ideally and normally, one must approach this task from the other end, so to speak. One does not begin confecting a homily and then set out in quest of something in literature that will advance and enhance the topic and its presentation. This would be facile. Rather it all begins at another, earlier time when one determines to cultivate a taste for and a habit of reading good literature. It is in the course of such reading that the inspirations will come to one for seeing connections between what he is now read-

---

6. I must not seem to make the relationships between literature and religion less complex than in fact they are. Some literature acts to confirm belief, e.g., the work of Tolstoy and T.S. Eliot, some literature challenges and seeks even to disconfirm belief, e.g., the writing of Jean-Paul Sartre, still other literature tends to induce belief e.g., the work of Paul Valery. As I assert elsewhere in this article, I believe that literature even when adversative to religion has uses for the preacher.

ing and some truth of life and faith that he may take in hand for a homily at some later time. The alert and conscientious homilist will note these words down for a future, felicitous incorporation into a homily.

One can see from this that the process of mining literature in the interests of forceful homilies is a subtle, long-term, oblique and patient enterprise, yet one that can pay the highest dividends.

If one were to inquire about the dynamics of recourse to literature, I should say that it serves at least to clarify the preacher's message, to italicize it, to help relate it to life experience. Literature is, after all, a kind of barometer of what people think and feel in a particular age.

Let me offer an example or two. It is hard to imagine a more striking way of concluding a homily on the easy accessibility of God than to cite William Blake on this topic:

> I give you the end of a golden string;
> Only wind it into a ball
> It will lead you in at heaven's gate,
> Built in Jerusalem's wall.[7]

A further example: in writing about the heroism of Father Damien, Robert Louis Stevenson magnificently gathers together all that one could want to say about total dedication to relieving human needs. His words might well be used to sum up a preacher's discussion of Christian compassion.

> Crowded with abominable deformities of our common manhood, a population such as surrounds us in the horror of a nightmare . . . Damien went there, and shut to with his own hand the door of his own sepulcher, and made his great renunciation, and slept that first night under a tree with his rot-

---

7. William Blake, "The Golden String."

ting brethren, alone with pestilence, and looking forward with what courage (with what pitiful shrinkings of dread God only knows) to a lifetime of dressing sores and stumps.[8]

One must not suppose that the literary allusion is used only to resay a point in other, more distinguished rhetoric. Sometimes the use of literature can be made to function by contrast. So for instance one could, I judge, very effectively begin a homily on the basic optimism of the Christian faith and life by citing those dour words of Mark Twain which bespeak his dark perspective on the human life experience.

> The burden of pain, care, misery grows heavier year by year; at length ambition is dead; longing for release is in their place. It comes at last—the only unpoisoned gift earth ever had for them—and they vanish from a world where they were a mistake and a failure and a foolishness; where they left no sign that they ever existed—a world which will remember them for a day and forget them forever.[9]

How bleak an assessment of the human life experience, how desperately at variance with the Christian view of life.

Again, one could bring home powerfully to an audience the sublimity and warmth of the Christian belief in the resurrection by setting it in contrast to the unrelieved despair about living beyond death that is reflected in the Gilgamesh epic.

> Whither are you roving, Gilgamesh
> the life you pursue you shall not find.
> For when the gods created mankind
> death for mankind they set aside,
> life in their own hands retaining.

---

8. Robert Louis Stevenson, "The Life of Father Damien."
9. Mark Twain.

> So, Gilgamesh, let your belly be full.
> Make merry by day and by night.
> Make of each day a feast of rejoicing.
> Day and night, dance and play.[10]

One must agree that these sentiments are not nearly as comforting as the Christian "Vita mutatur non tollitur."

In kindness to the hearer, one ought to foreswear a literary reference which has only a tenuous link with the preacher's message or none at all. Such a reference is being used crassly—just to entertain. The audience is left wondering how to make a connection between a quotation and the homily which in fact cannot be made. When that happens the point of the homily is clouded, the people are confused and the preacher has lost ground.

I should also counsel a sparing use of literary citation—a single such allusion within a homily of moderate length. Multiplicity can bedazzle the listener if it is over-rich.

To avail oneself of profane literature in order to support or enliven one's presentation of the Christian message is to stand in a noble and long-standing tradition, one that goes back at least to the Pauline correspondence where in several places one is made to hear the echo of secular writers e.g., Epimenides in Titus 1:12 and Menander in 1 Corinthians 15:33. A more explicit instance is found in Acts 17:28 where Luke depicts Paul as citing a line from the poet Aratus. Demonstrably there is good precedent for the Christian preacher today who seeks to draw power for his proclamation of the message from secular literature.

---

10. James B. Pritchard, ed., *Ancient Near Eastern Texts,* Princeton University Press (Princeton, 1969), p. 90.

THE SILENCED MAJORITY NEEDS TO COME TO WORD

Elisabeth Schüssler Fiorenza

> Elisabeth Schüssler Fiorenza holds two graduate degrees, a licentiate in pastoral theology and a doctorate in New Testament studies. At the University of Notre Dame she is professor of New Testament studies and theology but is currently on leave by virtue of a Guggenheim research scholarship. She has already made a number of significant contributions with her exegetical writings and during her leave is doing a commentary on the Book of Revelation. Her most recent book is "In Memory of Her: A Feminist Theological Reconstruction of Christian Origins." Without the insights of her chapter this book on preaching would be seriously lacking.
>
> At this moment of history, only men are allowed to preach in Roman Catholic pulpits. For this reason most of the authors in this volume are male. While it is not within the province of our book to discuss the pros and cons of that Church discipline, we felt that something should be said especially for the benefit of the men who are the preachers of today's Church.
>
> We found that message in a fine book published last year by Michael Glazier, Inc. called *A New Look at Preaching*. It is a compilation of the addresses and responses delivered at the First National Ecumenical-Theological Symposium on preaching. One of the distinguished speakers was Elisabeth Schüssler Fiorenza, biblical scholar and feminist theologian from Notre Dame. With her permission and the permission of the publisher, we are including a portion of her address. She was responding to a paper by Walter J. Burghardt; we urge you to read both in their entirety. We are pleased to include these portions because they provide an extremely valuable insight for the preacher.

Dr. Burghardt addresses foremost the homilist and his God-experience. His movement from study to experience to proclamation entails three major components; the first is study, the third and last is proclamation. The interlocking link in his proposal is experience. Experience is so to speak the missing link between study and proclamation. How does Father Burghardt understand experience? It is defined as the "experience of God, the experience of God's people and the experience of God's wonderful works." God's people are not the subject of experience but are here conceived of as a part of the object of the homilist's experience. Moreover he maintains that in order to preach the homilist must not just know something *about* God. Experience is specified as the homilist's experience *of* God, and it is this almost mystical experience of God that provides the link between study and proclamation. The homilist's experience is paradigmatic for Christian God-experience today.

Yet some of the major insights of recent theology stem from the application of the sociology of knowledge to theology. Raw experience or even common experience does not exist, but what exists are particular and individual experiences. All human experience insofar as it is human experience is bound to particular historical situations, is bound to specific cultural contexts, and is determined or at least influenced by the individual's social status and professional role in society and Church. This social conditioning of experience holds true also for the human experience of God. There is not an abstract common experience of God, but human experience of God is a particular experience that reflects and is shaped by its historical conditions in time and space, in culture and gender socialization. It is for this reason that I think it is important to look at experience not just as a link but also as a starting point of the movement from study to proclamation. The conditioning of experience poses the hermeneutical circle: Where do we begin? How do we reflect upon our own experiences? How do we become conscious of our own presuppositions? How do we articulate our assumptions? How do we make explicit our institutional commitments?

My own critical starting point is not that of the homilist or the ordained cleric but that of the proverbial "woman in the pew," the silenced majority. Whereas the experience of God and more and more also the study of Scripture and theology is open to all persons who are religious and call themselves Christians—and not just to those who are called "religious"—this is not the case for proclamation. Whereas all the people of God—clergy and lay, men and women, rich and poor—can experience God's grace and presence in their lives, proclamation is limited in the Roman Catholic Church by law to celibate male clergy only. For all practical purposes women of the past and of the present have not preached and are in many Christian churches still excluded from defining the role of proclamation in terms of their own experience. In such an ecclesiastical situation the danger exists that the homily will not articulate the experience of God as the rich and pluriform experience of God's people, but that the male preacher will articulate his own experience and will declare and proclaim his own particular experience as the experience of God *par excellence*. What is limited and particular to his experience will be proclaimed as universal and paradigmatic for everyone. I would, therefore, suggest that in such a restrictive ecclesial situation the homilist has not just the function to articulate his own experience of God as a very particular experience but must also seek to articulate publicly the learning processes and the experience of the people of God as well, since they are for the most part excluded from public proclamation. In order to be able to do so the homilist must (1) become self-critical, (2) be attentive to the experiences of others not like himself, (3) seek the involvement of those others in the task of preaching and proclamation, and (4) develop dialogical modes and styles of preaching.

(1) *Self-Critical:* To the extent that the homilist is aware of the hermeneutical circle he will become more and more self-critical. When he becomes aware of how experiences are embedded within a tradition, culture and society, the self-critical homilist will be on the alert not to substitute his own experience for that of the people of God, but rather seek to uncover the limitations of his own perspective and standpoint. Quite often I have heard sermons

about the insecurity wrought among the faithful by Vatican II, where it was obvious that the problem was not that of the congregation but that of the preacher. I have listened, for instance, to sermons attacking the liberality of modern exegesis, especially, e.g., about the visit of the magi, only to puzzle the audience, only to accomplish a moralist reduction of the text rather than a fuller development of its Christological importance. I have patiently listened to diatribes against the desire for power, the lust after pride—sermons that may reflect male drives and sins but do not take into account the need of women to take control over their own lives or to be encouraged in their search for self-affirmation. I have listened to sermon after sermon denouncing our consumerist attitudes and self-serving wealth, sermons addressing the upper middle class members of the congregation but not those who struggle for economic survival. A homilist who has just returned sun-tanned from a vacation in Florida or Arizona is ill-equipped to preach against the consumerism of a suburban housewife who has not had a vacation for years.

(2) *Attentive to Others' Experience:* One of the best ways of becoming self-critical is to listen carefully to the experiences of others rather than to project one's problems and fears into them. Liberation theology appeals to Scripture in pointing out that God can be found especially among the poor, the disadvantaged, the alienated, among those who do not belong. This does not mean that the poor and alienated are the objects of our charity and pastoral care so that they receive from us out of the superabundance of our goods and wisdoms. But rather it means that we are to listen to their experiences of God, to their analysis of how our values, life-style and pious self-security have led to and may have contributed to their exploitation and powerlessness, to their frustration and alienation, and may be the cause of their alienation from Christian faith and community. The homilist becomes self-critical when in such an attentive learning and listening process he becomes convinced that his own private experience is not the her-

meneutical key to the experience of God, or that he, as ordained, is not hermeneutically privileged in regard to the wisdom of Christ, but rather that this hermeneutical key is to be found with the poor, the disprivileged and the alienated. Only by becoming attentive to the God-experiences of "others" who are not "like him" will the homilist become capable of relativizing his own stance and of connecting his own experience with the God-experience of others. Only then will he become capable of articulating the God-experiences of the people of God today in a fuller sense.

A recent experience may illustrate this. Just this Christmas I listened to a sermon in a Brooklyn parish in which the homilist complained that today we talk too much about the "brotherhood of men" but neglect to speak about the "Fatherhood of God." Obviously this preacher never listened to women who have become alienated from the Church and from God because of sexist language that erases them as subjects from the public discourse and liturgy of their Church. He has never listened to the agony of women who need a whole week to recover their faith and hope after listening to a chauvinistic sermon on Sunday. I am sure that a great number of the women present did not notice or pay much attention to such androcentric preaching. Yet what about the ten or twenty percent who, like my daughter, are very conscious of the sin of sexism and no longer find themselves addressed by, or tolerant of, such male biased language and proclamation?

(3) *Involvement of "Others" in Proclamation:* Since no one single person can comprehend the multiform experience of the people of God or do justice to their legitimate religious needs, the homilist must seek to involve others in the move from experience to study to proclamation. Various models exist for such an involvement. Eduard Schwiezer, a Swiss New Testament scholar and pastor, invites a group of parishioners to discuss and prepare the homily. Ernesto Cardenal has given us the scriptural dialogues of the peasants in Nicaragua. The *Gospel of Solentiname* teaches us how poor and alienated people can understand the meaning of

the Gospel better than many highly trained middle-class exegetes do. This is not surprising because the New Testament Scriptures are rooted in the early Christian counter-cultural movement that was carried on for the most part by poor, alienated and disenfranchised people.

However, partial involvement of the people of God in the preparation for proclamation does not suffice. The impoverishment of preaching today is not due to the lack of able preachers, but to a structural clericalism which demands that one, single group of Christians—the ordained—articulate the richness and fullness of all Christians' God-experiences today. What is necessary is that more and more people, with a variety of life-experiences, not only are allowed to study the Scriptures and theology but also to become involved in proclamation. Relinquishment of his prerogatives as a homilist so that others can preach may be for the ordained preacher the best way of proclaiming God in our midst today.

The involvement of the laity in preaching does not just rest on an extraordinary gift of the Spirit or in an extraordinary situation, but is rooted in the God-experience of all the baptized. If ordination traditionally gives the power to preach, today the ordained homilist may be called to relinquish power over the laity; today such power must be reconceptualized not as power over others but as enabling power. Such an understanding of power is rooted in the words of Jesus and explored today especially by feminist theology. While the ordained is responsible that the word of God is proclaimed, such responsibility does not require that he himself always preach but that he enable others to do so.

(4) *The Style of Proclamation:* Such a communal understanding of proclamation as the right of all the people of God calls into question the "authoritarian one way form" of communication that characterizes preaching today. After lectures we have responses, after press conferences we have questions, but no one and nothing can challenge and question the proclamation of the

homilist. Dialogue homilies that engage the congregation in conversation or communal homilies that engage the congregation in a meditative sharing of experiences and insights are not necessarily "an adding up of zero to zero that equals zero," as someone once suggested, but they are serious attempts to develop a different, more ecclesial rather than clerical style of preaching. We must much more seriously rethink our form and means of proclamation and search for new modes of communication if the homily is to become open to critical dialogue and public discernment of how God can be experienced today in our midst. . . .

CONCLUSION: THE MOVE FROM EXPERIENCE TO PROCLAMATION

In a last step, I want to illustrate how my emphasis on experience as the primary ingredient in the move from study to proclamation would complement, concretize and broaden Father Burghardt's emphasis on experience and his homiletic suggestions. In his example of how he moves from study to proclamation, he not only carefully describes five steps in the preparation of a homily, but also focuses on the selection of the topic on Mary as the dominating figure of Advent. He informs us that the social location of the homily is the Shrine in Washington and that his choice of the topic was made with a view to the feast of the Immaculate Conception and in the light of a statement of Raymond Brown that three persons, Isaiah, Mary and John the Baptist, dominate the Advent liturgy. Mary reveals, according to him, more remarkably than anyone else how Christians should wait for Christ.

After having selected the topic and studied the Scriptures, Professor Burghardt moves to stage four that reflects on the details and organization of the homily and the religious response that the homily should call forth. After the study of Scripture and theology, one expects that he would connect the topic of the homily with his own or other people's religious experiences. Indeed, in this context he states that he pauses to read Shakespeare, Gerard Manley Hopkins, T.S. Eliot, and Tennessee Williams, and to listen to Beethoven, Barber, Tschaikovsky and even a dash of country music. He listens to the poets and musicians of his culture in order to formulate the details of the homily and to enflesh the topic. Yet I was surprised that he does not think of taking into account the experiences of pregnant women and their sense of self. I wonder whether the male poets and artists he mentions can give his sermon the detail, sensitivity, and insight that he would need for presenting the pregnant Mary of Nazareth as a paradigm of Christian Advent hope. Instead, listening to the experiences of women with pregnancy, their fears, hopes, troubles, and anxieties, their various experiences in giving birth and their exhilaration in touching the newborn child might have illumined and concretized our understanding of Advent waiting. Yet listening to individual experience does not suffice. One would also need to study feminist analyses, e.g., Adrienne Rich's book on the institution of motherhood in patriarchal society, to learn how the experience of motherhood is structurally and societally mediated and conditioned. One might also listen to single mothers on welfare or to the women at the checkout counter trying to feed and clothe their children. If the word has to become flesh in the homily, then it must become flesh in the particular experiences of those about whom the homily speaks. And the Mary of Advent is the pregnant Mary, the unwed mother.

This is not to criticize Father Burghardt's way of procedure—indeed more sermons should reflect such high literary standards and artistic sources. My point is mainly to emphasize the importance of reflecting upon and listening to different experiences, especially those pertinent to the theme of the sermon. Moving from such attentive listening to women's personal and structural experiences with motherhood, the Lukan texts on Mary come to new life. Mary, and not Joseph, is the morally responsible agent in becoming pregnant. The Gospel stresses her freedom of choice. She does not remain isolated but seeks support from another woman, Elizabeth. She has to learn that not natural family bonds and the claims of motherhood but the issues of God determine her relationship to her child. Her calling is not just motherhood but creative discipleship. As such a spirit-filled person, the pregnant Mary announces the future of God to the heavy laden and downtrodden in the Magnificat. The future of God's salvation and wholeness is not to be awaited passively and without our active involvement, but it is being born among us today from our flesh and blood, from our commitments and our struggles today. It is fashioned and becomes form as the hope for those who are without hope. In short, it is by articulating the pertinent experiences of women as the people of God that this homily on the Mary of Advent can elicit the faith response that the homily intends.

These brief remarks do not mean in any way to detract from the persuasiveness of Father Burghardt's suggestions, but they merely seek to underline how the interpretation of present and past experience demands that the homilist becomes acutely aware that not he himself, and not he alone, but, in many cases, others, may have the key to what the meaning of the word of God is for us today. It was in this light that I have suggested that an interpretation of Mary's experience during Advent can only take place with references to the personally and structurally reflected experiences of women among God's people. In short, the "silenced majority" must be heard and allowed into "speech" again if the richness and fullness of God's presence with us should be articulated and proclaimed today. The right of the baptized to proclamation is not just charismatic and extraordinary, but it must become the essential ingredient of all preaching, if the experience of God in our midst should be proclaimed in its fullness. While the ordained have the call and duty to ensure that proclamation takes place, all the people of God—ordained or not—are called to proclaim the great and marvelous deeds of God in Christ for our world and Church.

Part II

Camera

PSYCHOLOGICAL PERSPECTIVE
Neil Mahoney

> Rev. Neil Mahoney is a priest of the Archdiocese of Newark, N.J. where he works for Catholic Community Services. He has parish experience, mostly in the inner city, and recently completed a term as director of New Jersey Boystown. He has a theological degree from the Gregorian University in Rome as well as a doctorate in counseling from Fordham University. He is a skilled preacher, but we asked Doctor Mahoney to put on his psychologist cap and bring that expertise to his reflection on the preaching endeavor.

When we approach the pulpit to proclaim the "good news," we continue a tradition rooted in the gentle words and enthralling stories of Jesus himself. The congregation calls out to us as the eunuch to Philip: "How can I understand unless someone will give me the clue?" (Acts 8:30). In each century preachers have assumed the responsibility of making God's word alive and understandable to the people.

Dare we celebrate our own efforts in the post-Vatican II Church at preaching and making God's word "alive and understood"? Andrew Greeley gives us cause to squirm. It seems that indeed it has gotten "uncomfortable" in the pew; satisfaction with the quality of sermons has diminished drastically. A recent survey of preaching indicated that thirty-seven percent of the homilies had no applications of the teaching presented, and they were often too general and at times platitudinous. The complaint of Catholics was that much preaching does not touch their daily lives, their work, their marriage and family life, technology, leisure, unemployment, politics and education. The homilies often evidenced a "distance, a coldness; emotions of the spirit were lacking."[1]

If we were to accurately read the "signs of the times," it would appear that we are experiencing not a golden flowering of preaching, but rather a disheartened and uncertain preacher.

From whence will come the "boldness and openness" of Paul and Barnabas?

An essential element in the growth during psychotherapy is that the client first identify and acknowledge the problem. We, as preachers, are beginning to do that. Perhaps we have not been sensitive enough to the life experiences of our congregation, in a sense aloof and lacking in "emotions of the spirit." Maybe our own educational and religious formation was so highly structured that it allowed little room for personal searching and reflection upon one's own unique journey. It might be of help to us to attend to some basic psychological dynamics at work when we are preaching. In this chapter what I hope to do is help analyze the experience of both the congregation and the preacher with a view toward more powerful and effective preaching.

In applying psychology to preaching, one is *not* promoting a self-image psychology with evangelistic fervor. The preacher is not meant to become Dale Carnegie. He is not trying to reinforce secular materialism through a quasi-religious Gospel. The good news is the good news and that is what we preach. The preacher's sole purpose is to help unfold the mystery of Christ, to speak of Jesus' suffering and death, to make real his presence in our lives today. Psychology is at the service of this mission.

A basic assumption will be that any preacher can improve his preaching ability with training and a heightened sensitivity to some of the interacting variables at work between preacher and listener. The task of the preacher is to respond to the crises and

---

1. Leo R. Sands, "Preaching Since the Council," *Homiletic and Pastoral Review*, June 1982, p. 8.

questions of our day, to respond in ways that take into account the life experience of the congregation.

CONGREGATION AS PARTNER

The psychological interplay between preacher and congregation is enormous. In fact, the congregation enters into a partnership which most influences the outcome of any communication. Listening is not a passive activity. Even the most relaxed form of listening, e.g., in response to music, involves *doing* something. The "listener" brings to his listening behavior a lifetime of experience. The listener will then process the message being received in a great variety of different contexts. The listener responds to the occasion (a wedding, a funeral), to the weather (a bleak rainy day), to immediate life crises (unemployment). In each of these many different situations, a slightly different set of perceptions and responses may be elicited. The preacher then approaches a sea of interacting stimuli.

The congregation forms an image of the preacher which has far more impact on their response than any logical statements and lofty sentiments he may be expounding upon. While the images formed of you as preacher are as numerous as the listeners in the congregation, I would suggest one important stimulus emanating from the preacher. The listener asks: Is this preacher communicating a warmth and interest in me? Surely a preacher perceived to be distant, cold, and lacking in spirit is never going to achieve his purpose of unfolding the mystery of Christ. People want to perceive in the preacher a sincerity and concern for their lives. In settings in which congregations remain stable, such as the parish, the preacher's broader involvement in their lives will affect their attentiveness and desire to "believe as the preacher believes." Knowledge of the preacher's compassion for the sick, leadership of youth, honesty in relationships will all be ingredients to forming an image of the speaker. Simply stated, the life of the preacher is a powerful variable in the hearing of the homily. The congregation is responding to the perceived speaker. Perception is the reality!

The chemistry of the interaction between the preacher and audience is paralleled to some degree in a recent Broadway play. Kathy Bates plays a daughter determined to commit suicide in the play, " 'Night Mother." In an interview she described the alchemy of emotions that occurs as a different conglomeration of people and feelings and ideas and issues and backgrounds all come into one space with their own spirituality. We would do well to sensitize ourselves as preachers to what the dramatic artist has long perceived to be the "alchemy of emotions" that builds between audience and artist. It is the interest and attention of the listener that helps shape the preacher. As preachers we respond to the listeners' reactions whether they be perceived as positive encouragement or bored disinterest. The preacher may become more fired up about the message, or perhaps hesitate, adjust glasses, look at notes. In response to the experience of audience feedback, the preacher may change the pace of delivery, adjust vocal tone, use more gestures. Whether perceptibly or imperceptibly, the preacher changes!

At a funeral of a friend's father, I was vividly reminded of the impact of the congregation's attention and interest. Desiring to say something meaningful and consoling, I worked hard in preparation of the homily. By my own humble evaluation, the message was right on target. As I began the homily, my friend started squirming in the front row and then began a conversation with her husband and then her daughter. The entire congregation focused in on this commotion and it became all-consuming. Having lost everyone, my consoling words totally ignored, I stopped. The variable that I was trying to so blithely ignore had finally halted me. The chief mourner was in dire need of a rest room and not the preacher's brilliant words of consolation. A pointed reminder that the "active listener" does influence preaching behavior. In psychotherapy, you will probably say more to the therapist you perceive to be an interested listener. As a preacher, you are likely to "give" more to a congregation you perceive to be receptive.

No matter how lofty the message or dynamic the presentation, it is all lost unless the hearer is "attending" to it. Listening is a process of focusing our sensory receptors upon the stimulus, in this case, the spoken word and bodily gestures.

A listener cannot give *continuous* attention. Attention is generally sporadic and can be held for a limited time span. This general principle militates against lengthy homilies. To hold attention, it is important that the preacher be more concrete (thus the success of the storyteller!) rather than conceptually abstract. As stated earlier, the listener brings his experiences to the hearing of the message. It is by relating to the experiences of the congregation that we gain their attention. Our experiences survive not as abstractions but as memories of concrete things that we have seen and heard.

A mere repeating of the Gospel story will produce little or no communicative effect. The preacher is called upon to help the listener interpret this experience, this journey in the light of Christ. The preacher must speak of what is familiar to the listener and help move the listener to what is new in experiencing the presence and love of God. What we are looking to do is to translate experience into a language that is both understandable and appealing. St. Francis told stories; we are rediscovering the power of the story. In some ways we must be an actor, an illustrator, an image creator. In speaking to our congregation, we must use words that people can see— "clouds of despondency," Jesus dying in the midst of "tears and thunder," a mourner with vision "blinded by tears." We are looking to communicate an excitement about what we say, to take the experience of the listener and give it new meaning.

KNOWING THE CONGREGATION

In extolling the virtues of illustrious preachers such as St. Paul, Francis of Assisi, Bishop Sheen, and Dr. Martin Luther King, what we admire ultimately was their "adaptability." They could take the "good news" and make it come alive for their congregation. It takes a mentally healthy preacher to adjust, to respond to the needs of today while remaining true to the tradition and kerygma message.

The preacher must know his audience. Effective preaching is likely to occur if the preacher takes into account the listener's frame of reference and adapts his approach to the listener's perspective. We must get to know their beliefs, values, motives, and viewpoints. This is not pop psychology or watered-down ethical-cultural philosophy. It is the purpose of preaching to introduce Christ in ways that will make the congregation truly active listeners.

It requires patience and effort to know your congregation. One of America's best known speakers, William Jennings Bryan, came to a community where he would be speaking in order to look around and to talk to as many locals as possible. He wanted to know their interests and views. He wanted to be influenced by this information and to incorporate it. Ultimately, he wished to speak to their "experience," to be perceived as "one" with them.

To whom are *we* preaching? Our congregations are being gently persuaded by the sophisticated packaging of Häagen-Dazs ice cream. Dare we present our "product" in language that is colorless, lifeless? Our youth's mores are being shaped by *Flashdance, Fast Times at Ridgemont High,* and *Porky* (unlimited). How can we ignore in our preaching these young people confronted with choices unknown to us from a different generation? Our Catholicism drives Captain Furillo of *Hill Street Blues* to seek forgiveness in confession for a breach of ethics in convicting a criminal, while at the same time finding consolation in the privacy of his lover's passionate embrace. Our children are stimulated by the *Sesame Street* panoply of educational entertainment. Finally, our youth turned on by the sound and fury of disco have found a new thrill in surreal video accompaniment. Into all of this enters the preacher!

In order to adapt, the preacher must know and analyze his own audience. My own style, language, and manner of speaking changed drastically coming from a middle class white parish to an urban black setting. Another adaptation was called for when I was invited to speak at a parish recollection day on Mid-Life Crises. I prepared well and arrived to find an audience with a mean age of seventy, the proverbial "remnant." Needless to say, I did some very fast adapting. The preacher who remains unchanged by his congregation more than likely will not be listened to. Every new audience can be a stimulus for drawing out of the preacher untapped wisdom, untouched love, and even vulnerability.

A SHARED EXPERIENCE

There is probably no more important dimension to the preaching experience than finding the "common ground," the shared experience with the congregation. Listeners are psychologically more open to speakers who are perceived as being "in the same boat." When Dr. King emerged from the long dusty roads of marching and the prisons of human hate, his message had far greater credibility.

Before a word is even uttered, perceptions of the preacher are already being formulated by the listener. An audience of divorced parents would initially be more receptive to a speaker known to have experienced the trauma of divorce and the burden of single parenthood. A priest known to have served faithfully in a parish for a number of years would at least initially be attended to more by a group of priests than a social worker with no pastoral experience. Simply stated, the audience responsivity is to some extent dependent upon the preacher being perceived as sharing common life experiences. It is no accident that political speakers will don the most bizarre symbols (e.g., hard hat) in order to clearly communicate: "I am one with you!"

What the preacher must do is find that common ground with the congregation. Knowing the audience and feeling a genuine caring for the audience makes it far more likely that the shared experience will be communicated.

Let St. Paul give us an example of finding common ground. St. Paul (Acts 17:16) while at Athens was exasperated to see how the city was full of idols. (He, a Christian; they, pagan—no common ground for preaching?) When brought into court and asked to explain his strange ideas, Paul didn't attack their idolatry and thus make them inaccessible as listeners. Paul began by complimenting: "Men of Athens, I see that in everything that concerns religion you are uncommonly scrupulous." Paul then establishes some common ground: "As I was going round looking at the objects of your worship, I noticed an altar bearing the inscription, 'To an Unknown God.' What you worship but do not know—this is what I now proclaim." Whether Paul succeeded or not is unimportant and revolves more on the Spirit than cleverness, but what he does model is the need to establish yourself on some common ground with your audience.

Self-disclosure is another avenue to establishing a common bond with the congregation. In my own training I can remember being taught to *never* use the pronoun "I" and to never talk about yourself—the people don't want to hear about you! There is a balance to be achieved. Appropriate self-disclosure has the benefit of increasing trust and attraction. People can relate to a story about your niece, a painful moment in your life, good news in your life. Self-disclosure can bring greater consistency between your self-concept and the congregation's concept of you. However, there is a subtle ban on self-disclosure in our society—the fear of not being macho, or of being exhibitionist, or just plain weak. Certainly we are not advocating pulpit ego trips, weekly bleeding in front of the congregation or scandalous revelations. At the same time we should not say *never* to self-disclosure. The appropriate use of personal experience communicates to the congregation that yes, indeed, we do share a common ground; yes, we are making this journey of faith together.

We have explored some of the important psychological elements to the preaching experience. A recognition of the active listener helping "shape us" should help free us from a rigidity that ignores the life experience of those to whom we preach. The effort at knowing the listeners, their joys and sorrows, fears and hopes for tomorrow should enable us to speak in ways that help place their experience in relation to an ever-present God. The desire on our part to unite ourselves and become "as one" with those who make the journey along with us should spare us the appearance of being lacking in "emotions of the spirit."

While we all know the experience of preaching in a way that leaves us feeling empty and totally ineffectual, we have also had the experience of touching someone's heart and communicating God's love. While there are a sea of variables interacting between preacher and congregation, such as image, perception, and adaptability, there remains one immeasurable variable: the power of the Holy Spirit.

TOUCHING PEOPLE'S HEARTS

Patricia Hickman Livingston

> Patricia Hickman Livingston is a counselor and author but is best known as a lecturer and communicator. She gives workshops, courses and keynote addresses to audiences covering a wide spectrum, in the business community as well as church circles. She belongs in this volume because she has an uncanny ability to communicate effectively with priest groups. A regular member of the Notre Dame Clergy Institute faculty, she has worked in seminaries and religious houses of men and women, as well as traveling over the world to bring her message to military chaplains. Here she writes of touching hearts, and when you have finished her chapter, you will realize that Mrs. Livingston practices what she preaches.

Last summer the world was introduced to a skinny, huge-eyed, wrinkled being from another planet named Extra Terrestrial. In the final scene of the film, E.T. is leaving to go back home and must say goodbye to Elliot, the boy he has come to love deeply. As he stands looking at the boy before turning to go, he puts his long, bony finger to his heart and says "Ouch." Everyone in the audience who has ever loved and had to let go understood that pain. It hurts to leave someone you love.

E.T.'s gesture is the same as the metaphor we use in our language for the evoking of feeling: the touching of the heart.

When Frank McNulty asked me to write this chapter, he suggested I write about something we have talked about many times over the years, something we have teamed up and tried to do together, the touching of hearts.

The heart is a symbol for our feelings, for our emotional life, for our deepest humanness. It is an image for the source of relatedness, of energy toward life, of what the Greeks called eros.

I think one of the most important functions of preaching is

heartening. Preaching comes from the Latin *praedicare,* to proclaim or make known. The best of preaching, to my mind, happens when the speaker proclaims or makes known something that enables people to take heart, something that encourages them. (I like recalling that the Latin root of courage is *cor* meaning heart.)

Life is hard for most of us—often uncertain, puzzling, and wearying as we go about the difficult work of being responsible despite unforeseen demands and disappointment, of trying, in the midst of shifting times and values, to be faithful to our commitments. It involves facing illness and failure and loss of love, the death of dreams and the darkening of hope. It means learning to accept once and for all what my great aunt once said to me on a porch swing in a Kentucky summer, "There's just not *ever* a perfect situation, Honey."

In the face of *that,* all of us need heartening. We need a healing connection with the source of life; we need truth that helps make sense of difficulties and takes us to the Love-beyond-knowing that lies deep within.

For preaching to hearten it must offer both thought and feeling. The thought offers clarity and direction; the feeling brings depth and power. First, then, there needs to be an idea, a thought, a concept at the center of the talk or homily through which people can better understand life, a truth that can illuminate their experience and enable them to claim it as meaningful and honorable.

The explanation of the thought is only part of what makes that claiming happen. A concept can be expounded and the people can have an objective interest, a rational acknowledgement, but it may never reach the level on which they live, and may be gone before they drive out of the parking lot. It is necessary not just to explain the idea, but to somehow engage them, to touch their hearts, to add feeling to the thought.

There are two key ingredients for touching people's hearts, presence and concreteness. Presence involves a personal presence both to the group and to the material. Being present to the group is expressed through some kind of greeting in the beginning, then through eye contact, responsiveness, and expression while speaking. This communicates that the homily is not something one-sided or mechanical, but an exchange between persons.

When as a speaker you are present to your material it means that what you are saying is something that has real meaning for you. It is some aspect of the truth of life that has had some personal impact, has made a difference to you as you live out your life of faith in all its humanness. If it comes from your heart, it is very likely to touch the hearts of others. As John Henry Cardinal Newman reflected, "Cor ad cor loquitur"—heart speaks to heart.

I recently met a delightful Paulist priest who has for some time been teaching seminarians and deacons to preach. He said that he is constantly criticizing their homilies because they have no real connection with life.

"For whom are you writing that?" he asked one seminarian who had written a forceful denunciation of the sin of pride. "Look out at the people. Do you see anyone out there who really looks like his big problem is pride? Most of these poor jokers would benefit from a little pride. They are harder on themselves than anyone. And what about you? You have no idea how special you are. The last thing I can imagine endangering you is pride. Preach out of your own experience. If it is really meaningful to you, it will be meaningful for them, too."

Each of us has a personal stock of meaning, of truth that life has taught us. None of us will ever grasp all there is to know, be wise in all the ways of wisdom. Truth is too vast. The best that we can contribute is our particular understanding from our own experience.

Years ago a Jesuit friend shared a fantasy with me of how the Creed might have been written. He saw it not as a list that all the apostles had identically in mind, not as a cut and dried number of tenets, but as a pooling of what each one deeply believed. He imagined a scene like this:

> "How about you, John?" Peter or Luke or whoever was organizing it might have said. "What do you believe?"
>
> "Hey, that's good, yes, write that down. . . . Now, James, what about you?"
>
> "Right! Absolutely! That should definitely go in there, don't you all think so?"

He imagined that one by one they said what meant the most to them, what they felt committed to, what seemed crucial and central to them, and at the end of it they had the Creed.

To touch hearts, the central thought of your preaching must come from some aspect of *your* truth, some idea that really seems to you worth proclaiming.

Sometimes this is not easy to come up with. It may be suggested by the readings or the occasion. Sometimes, however, there is nothing there that you can connect with, that you feel any presence to, any excitement about. It might then be helpful to take some time to reflect on your recent days: to look for what has engaged you, what has made you think, or caused you to swear under your breath, or saddened you, or given you a good laugh. Was there an incident with someone, or a line from a letter, or a scene from a film, or a view out your window? Where was there freshness for you? The sense of freshness can lead you to something that you feel present to, and that may offer the key to what you can preach on that will touch people.

(Some times are really blah; sometimes *we* are really blah; there is no freshening; we don't feel much presence to anything. In those times it is invaluable to have a file or a drawer or a journal where we have kept notes or references to things that have touched us.)

Once you have selected an idea that you feel some presence to, the second key to heartening people is concreteness. It is essential to find a way to get the idea onto a personal level. There needs to be an example or illustration that translates from the abstract. Life never happens in general; it always takes place in the particular, always in a story. Through a story we can connect with the truth of the human condition and see that truth in our own story.

The parables in the Gospel are marvelous examples of this concreteness. Sometimes you can take a story right out of the readings. Instead, or in addition, you might use a story from your own life, or the life of someone you know. Or you might use something from literature or theater or film. The important thing is that it makes your main idea real, that it enfleshes it in life, and that it is a story you yourself are touched by. If it touches you, it will probably touch them.

As I have been writing this, I have been trying to select an example to use to demonstrate what I am talking about. In my years in various parish congregations, retreat groups, and conference audiences, I have heard many powerful homilies that have touched me deeply. I considered trying to reconstruct one of these.

It seemed to be more appropriate, however, to try to do what I have been describing—to try to pick out an idea that has a great deal of meaning for me and to concretize it with a story that touched me.

A truth about life that is very important to me is this: we *are* more than we *do*. Our worth as a person is not defined by our competence or our performance. We are not less lovable when we become less capable. The love of God is not something we earn. He loves us totally for ourselves, not for what we achieve.

This concept is easy enough to understand abstractly, but in practice it is very hard to live out. We feel worthless when we become sick or old or cannot do what we once did. We feel unlovable as a person when we fail at a task or make a bad mistake in a relationship.

Coming to forgive ourselves, to love ourselves when we have failed or lost our power to produce is hard. Coming to trust that God loves us utterly in our imperfection is a life task.

I recently watched my youngest son, Boo, go the first round with this learning.

I almost missed it. If I hadn't stumbled over his glove in the middle of the darkened family room, I would not have realized that he was lying there on the couch.

"When did you get back from practice?"

"A while ago." Almost inaudible.

"How did it go?"

Silence.

"Did it go O.K.?"

Silence. I waited what seemed like a long time.

"Again, this year I'm going to be on the bench until the last two innings, then play outfield."

I was shocked. This was his fifth year, the last in Little League. It was a humiliation after being on the team so long. He had been so sure that this year would be different, and had been hopeful in the practices that were leading up to the beginning of the season tomorrow night. I was furious at the coach. How could he! How could he! I just ached for Boo, feeling his pain, his embarrassment, his loss of self-esteem. I wanted to shout:

"Now you listen to me. You're worth more than that whole team and that stupid coach who can't see talent with a telescope!"

I wanted to say, "Baseball's not everything. Don't forget the great scores you made on the National Achievement Tests."

I wanted to give him my mother's classic defense against all pain: "Nothing can get you down. You're Irish."

And last of all I wanted to say: "I'm calling that coach right now and taking you off that team, and you can start taking tennis lessons."

But I didn't. I didn't say anything at all. I just sat there in the dark loving him, knowing that there are days when our self-esteem is measured by our batting average, and that those are days no one can help us with, except to stand with us until something deep within us fights back, saying: "I am more. I am much more. I am unique in all the world."

It was quiet a long time. "Do you want to say anything else, Boo?"

"No, I guess I'll turn in."

The next night was to be the first game. There was a final practice after school. He came home from it whistling, grabbing chocolate chip cookies with both hands. Instead of saying "Don't spoil your supper," I poured him a glass of milk and began as casually as I could: "How did practice go?" trying not to believe in some leprechaun's three wishes that had made him into the starting pitcher.

He laughed. "I did pretty crummy." A huge bite out of a cookie. "You know, the coach was right. I haven't been hitting too hot, and I'm not looking too good on the grounders. I need more practice. But I still want to play."

He walked off, depositing red clay from his cleats all the way across the kitchen with a spring in his step that said for sure that his self-worth was now distinct from his batting average again. He had survived the first of a lifetime of learnings that our performance is not what gives us value. At least for now he had answered back: "I am more."

I have tried to say what I think the key things in heartening are when you preach: presence to the people, presence to the idea, concreteness in the telling. I have suggested that if it has meaning for you, power and freshness, it will touch their hearts.

It usually does. Sometimes, however, you can be totally present, you can be very touched by what you are trying to say, and still no one responds. They don't understand it, or maybe aren't even listening.

I hope whether you are Irish or not, that it doesn't get you down. You have done what you could to offer your thought and feeling to be a channel for heartening. If you have some pain about it (as I always do) you might touch your heart and say "Ouch" softly when no one is looking—or maybe you might go and find someone who heartens you and have a cookie.

UNLOCKING THE IMAGINATION
Fred A. Baumer

> Rev. Fred A. Baumer is assistant professor of word and worship at Catholic Theological Union in Chicago. In this role he calculates that he hears a homily once every eighteen hours of his life. A member of the Society of the Precious Blood, he is degreed in theology and drama and will soon hold a doctorate in speech from Northwestern University. He is in great demand for preaching workshops and made a major contribution to the well received N.C.C.B. publication *Fulfilled in Your Hearing: The Homily in the Sunday Assembly*. Father Baumer is a man immersed in the theory and the practice and contributes often to the literature. Here he reflects on the role of imagination.

"What part of the person is being addressed when the community assembles for worship?" asks Patrick Collins in *More Than Meets the Eye*.[1] Collins argues that ritual primarily addresses the imagination of the participants, and, through imaginal forms such as music, dance, poetry and drama, creates "conditions of possibility for experiencing the Mystery of Christ, which is Christ in us, the Church."[2] Imaginal forms used in liturgy create the conditions whereby we encounter God.

The homily, defined as preaching within eucharistic ritual, also addresses the imagination. An integral part of ritual,[3] each homily constructs a linguistic contour in which mystery can somehow be present to the human situations of the people gathered for worship. The Sunday assembly may believe that God has acted in history, but often has real questions as to how God can be encountered in a world of inflationary spirals, disease, prejudice and alienation. The homilist names the community's situation in

---

1. Patrick W. Collins, *More Than Meets the Eye* (New York: Paulist Press, 1983), p. 13.
2. *Ibid.*, p. 14.
3. Cf. Vatican II, *Constitution on the Sacred Liturgy, #52.*

which they find themselves, identifying for them the attitudes or behavior contrary to faith. Then the preacher proclaims a Gospel vision derived from the lectionary passages that addresses an analogous situation. The preacher word-paints two pictures within the listener's imagination. One is the human situation where God is undisclosed, and the second is that same human situation in which God is revealed. The listener experiences these two linguistic contours in tension. A new synthesis must occur to resolve the tension. Insofar as the listeners experience God present in the resolution of this tension, they respond in praise and thanks.[4]

If eucharistic ritual and the homily are meant to creatively engage the listeners' imagination, what then is this faculty of the psyche? Each age from Plato to the present has attempted an answer. Imagination has come to stand for a variety of mental acts, from sense recall (imagine an elephant) to fantasy construction (imagine seeing through the eye of God). The nature of imagination, where it exists, and precisely how it operates are age-old questions outside the scope of this article.[5] The question under discussion here is how the homilist engages the listener's imagination.

The human mind stores sense data as it encounters reality, automatically associating new data with that gathered from previous experiences. Metaphorically, the databanks in which sense perceptions are stored can be envisaged as bodies of water. The purpose of the imagination is to act as the lock between two unrelated bodies of water. The imagination is a channel, a lock with no water of its own, that permits seemingly unrelated ideas to meet, flow together, and create a new body of water, a new synthetic understanding.

---

4. A fuller understanding of homily is given in *Fulfilled in Your Hearing: The Homily in the Sunday Assembly* (Washington, D.C.: USCC Publications, 1982).

5. An excellent study of religious imagination is Ray Hart, *Unfinished Man and the Imagination* (New York: Seabury Press, 1979), pp. 180–369.

By engaging the imagination, ritual preaching opens the locks between a human situation seemingly void of God's presence and an analogous Gospel situation in which God is active and present. Both situations are presented as linguistic contours of reality. In one the Kingdom that is not "of" this world but is "in" this world is absent; in the other it is active. The listeners recognize themselves in each linguistic contour, and must resolve the tension caused by the opening of the lock between the two linguistic bodies of water.

Here is an example. In the film *Jesus of Nazareth,* Franco Zeffirelli paints a film portrait of the homilist Jesus preaching in an indirect, poetic manner to the imagination of his listeners. The scene is a festive meal in the home of Matthew the tax collector (Lk 15). The film portrayal is sensuous. Jesus is feasting with Matthew. Fine food, good music and easy companionship are part of the environment. Peter stands outside the door, righteously indignant at the master's spending time with the disinherited Jew who collects taxes for the Romans. As a law-abiding practitioner of his faith, Peter would not cross that sinful threshold. The party begins to wear down. Jesus is begged for a story. He begins.

A prodigal father has two sons, one insolent and disobedient, a squanderer of his inheritance. Peter grins with righteousness, and Matthew hangs his head in recognition of himself in the figure of the younger son. Jesus continues, introducing an elder son at the end of the story—a son who insults his father by not taking part in the feast. Peter's grin fades. He recognizes himself as the one with no party in his soul, unwilling to forgive and feast.

In his story, Jesus creates a linguistic contour in which the imaginations of both Peter and Matthew are caught. Matthew recognizes his situation as that of the younger son, with the possibility of returning to the father. Peter acknowledges that he is the older son, with a new possibility for action than that which he thought the law prescribed. Zeffirelli directs the scene to a moving and apt conclusion by presenting Matthew and Peter slowly walking toward one another and embracing in the doorway.

The question arises as to how Zeffirelli constructed the film sequence after reading Luke 15. The scriptural text says that Jesus often ate with sinners and told stories at these meals. In his own imagination Zeffirelli constructed the rest, making the situation come alive in the real lives of people who may have been at such a dinner.

Homilists who prepare their preaching from scriptural readings are called upon to engage their own imaginations in the preparation process. They are asked to open the imaginative lock between the world of the 80's and the 1980's, so that worlds distinct in time, culture, and history can flow together creating a new possibility. Secondly, their Sunday morning delivery is an imaginative description of what happened to them in their imaginative preparation process. The homily then may present at least two linguistic contours in tension with one another that demand resolution in the listeners' imagination.

The first step for the preacher is to insure that the scriptural text gets a chance to speak its own meaning. Often the preacher begins the preparation of a homily by speedily skimming the Gospel text, asking: "What does the text mean?" In such a case a principle generally emerges: this text is about hospitality, or forgiveness, or persistence in prayer. Once the preacher decides the principle, the next step is application to contemporary experience. The third step then is exhortation to a new attitude or behavior.

The form of the homily using the above imageless preparation methodology develops through three stages.[6]

---

6. This tri-partite division is fully elaborated by William Skudlarek, in "Preaching and the Homily," an NCR cassette series, Kansas City, Missouri.

1. Today's Scripture tells us . . . (reduction of the meaning of the event described in the Scripture to a principle or truth).
2. This applies to our lives by . . . (prescriptive application of truth to people's lives).
3. Therefore we ought . . . (exhortation to new behavior).

There is nothing inherently wrong with such a methodology of preparation or form of delivery. Unfortunately it addresses the reason of the listeners and not their imagination. Such a process gives information, again useful, but the mere acquisition of information does not necessarily lead to transformation of attitude or behavior. No matter how much information the surgeon general gives, some cigarette smokers will not change their habits. Likewise, informative statistics do not buckle seat belts. We need to identify with the transformative power of information before we change.

An imaginative approach to scriptural texts is not beginning with "What does the text mean?" but with the question "How does the text feel when it speaks?" The preacher begins by reading the texts *aloud* several times, sounding the feelings of those who speak as well as trying to determine the meaning. When Jesus asks Peter "Do you love me?" three times, each time is spoken with a different set of feelings from Jesus. The questions are not merely an academic exercise to test Peter's fidelity, but come from real life feelings between these two men. Imaginative homilists will allow those feelings to surface within their own life experience, searching for an analogous situation in their contemporary community's life. What is occurring in the preparation process is the immediate opening of the lock between the affective-cognitive meaning of the scriptural texts and the existential life of the homilist.

After clarifying through commentaries, biblical dictionaries, and other critical sources, the homilists engage their imagination by opening the lock between the understanding and feelings of certain persons within the biblical story and themselves. Zeffirelli did this in preparation for filming the prodigal son story as recorded in Luke 15 by imaginatively becoming Peter and Matthew hearing the story.

For example in preparation for preaching on Luke 7, the story of Jesus having dinner with Simon the Pharisee at which a woman interrupts the banquet with her display of tears-washing and hair-drying Jesus' feet, the imaginative homilist will speak the story aloud several times not only to understand what is going on in the story, but to get a sense of how Jesus, Simon, the woman, and the other guests at the meal must have felt. Then, when Jesus tells his parable about the two men who owed money, one five hundred coins, the other, fifty, the imaginative homilist will feel how each person in the situation felt when the story was told.

In so doing this story may not only be about the generous forgiveness of God for the great sinners, but how each of us, great sinner or not, can always come back to God. I discovered in this process that the story was really about those of us who are not great sinners and never owe five hundred coins, but those who always owe fifty, and take for granted the one to whom we owe it, not seeing any need to wash feet, anoint with oil, or do the customary rituals that acknowledge our relationship with the gift-giver.

The form of this homily becomes something like this:

1. Our human situation is such that . . . (description of taking for granted the one to whom we owe a lot of little things).
2. The scriptural situation describes an interaction of God and his people such as . . . (description of the feelings of Simon who didn't feel that he had to treat the Master with any special respect).
3. Therefore I find . . . (description of the ambiguity in the preacher's own life at these two linguistic contours, with possible description of what the homilist will do about it).

What is available as source material for homilies in this second imaginative preparation and delivery form is all the lived experience of the homilist. Parables and Gospel narratives can never be reduced to principles or truths to be applied to life. Instead the homilists describe the unique human situation within their community that is analogous to the lived experiences described by the Scriptures. This description comes from the imaginative felt-sensing of the affective as well as cognitive meaning of the Scriptures. The homilists risk describing the difference that occurred in their own lives when they opened the locks between their own imaginative construction of reality and the Scriptures' rendition of an analogous situation.

In delivery, the listeners receive the descriptive utterance of what occurred through the imaginative interaction of text and life for the homilist. They hear the homilist paint linguistic contours of the Kingdom that is in their world but not yet of their world. In the tension that surfaces from imagining these two linguistic worlds, the possibility of a new, transforming order may happen in the minds of the listeners. They then will make their own decisions as to how to live out this new attitude. A description of how the preacher hopes to do it may be a guide for them, especially if the homilist is truly identified with their lives.

The homily, as ritual speech, encounters God in the imagination. I am reminded of a brief dialogue between Shaw's St. Joan and Robert, her first friend in her siege of Orleans.

Joan: I hear voices telling me what to do. They come from God.

Robert: They come from your imagination.

Joan: Of course. That is how the messages of God come to us.[7]

---

7. George Bernard Shaw, *St. Joan*, Scene 1.

THE RIGHT BRAIN LANGUAGE OF POWER

Clarence Thomson

> Clarence Thomson learned the theory of communication at the University of Ottawa where he received a master's degree. The practical has come from teaching homiletics to the deacons at the Center for Pastoral Life and Ministry in Kansas City and serving as director of Credence Cassettes for the National Catholic Reporter. In this latter job he has clocked thousands of hours listening to people communicating their messages. He has a second master's in theology and was editor of the resource guide for adult education published by the NCR. Mr. Thomson offers the practical conclusions of some recent research on the working of the brain.

When Cicero finished his orations, all Rome went about saying, "What a fine speech Cicero gave today." But when Demosthenes spoke, the Greeks said, "Let us march." Such is the difference between a good homily and preaching with power.

Being able to speak with power is to some degree simply an extension of one's personality, as in the case of a Luther, Augustine or Jesus himself.

However, there are some powerful techniques and insights that can release the power we do have. They are our concern here.

Two California researchers have learned startling and helpful information about the way our brains work in communication.

Roger Sperry at the California Institute of Technology received a Nobel Prize for this work on the differences between the two hemispheres of our brain. He learned that each hemisphere processes information in a strikingly different way.

The left brain, Sperry discovered, is logical, factual, sequential, with highly developed verbal capacity and prefers to have its information in a time sequence, one step at a time. The ultimate left brain technology is the computer. Spock in "Star Trek" is an example of what we'd all be like if we used just our left hemisphere.

The right half, or the right brain, as it is usually called, operates quite differently. It operates best off impressions, it uses intuition more than logic, it is sensitive to pattern rather than detail, and it organizes information in space rather than in time. When a coach describes the "great anticipation" some athletes have, he is describing someone who grasps things all at once, holistically. The right brain quarterback who is brilliant in a complex game is sometimes not very articulate afterward. He has strong right brain development but not strong left brain, verbal skill.

We all use both sides of our brain, and real creativity and real power is found only when we combine both sides. Most of us have one side that is dominant and we prefer the type of communication that goes with our dominance.

Paul Watzlawick at Stanford used this information to go a step further. He makes a convincing case that our language is hemispheric specific. By this he means that certain types of speech are addressed to the left brain and other forms are directed to and received by our right brain—and so are processed differently. This understanding can be helpful to the preacher.

Left brain speech has the advantage of being the clearer. An explanation in a text, the program of a computer, the rubrics of a papal ceremony are worthless if they are not clear. Most if not all of our education places an enormous value on clarity. It begins in the most primitive form when we come to school—the emphasis on neatness is a precursor of later devotion to clarity. Our left brain logic is developed from the beginning and our entire education system serves our left brain well.

On the other side, right brain language is not always clear, but it is the language of power. Right brain language has the ability to reinterpret an existing body of information in a new way.

Watzlawick says that the right brain language is the language of puns, double meanings, aphorisms, metaphors, jokes, stories—all the things we don't use and don't learn in a classroom. Students are seldom given a low grade on a test or term paper because they are boring, humorless or lacking in panache. If they are it is only in literature class, where such language is hermeneutically sealed off. We are systematically trained as fundamentalists, who confine the meaning of truth to what can be explained with the left brain language.

Religion shows a marked preference for the language of power, not of clarity, especially when the language is experiential and less expository. The language of dogma, of course, is left brain. The language of mystery is in the realm of the right brain.

This insight of hemispheric-specific language sheds some light on Jesus. The disciples complained that he spoke to them only in parables. He didn't do that just to be perverse or clever. He did it because parables have the power to convert. What he lost with the disciples in clarity, he gained in allegiance.

Some of the power of right brain language to change the hearer derives from the holistic preference of right brain thought. *Pars pro toto* is a familiar literary device, but one can draw from it some practical conclusions about conversion. If something—a piece of art or an attitude—is holistic, then the whole is contained in each part. Thus the way to make personal change is to address the right brain and persuade it to make a small but symbolic (holistic) change. Rather than making sweeping resolutions about a general problem, make a right brain appeal to a specific instance. For instance, instead of saying, "From now on, I will be more patient," say, "I will be patient with my friend who complains too much."

We seem to know this. Each year the media make fun of all those who think they can make New Year's resolutions. Of course, if you make resolutions the usual way, they are doomed, because we are trained to use a highly systematic generalized approach. We can grit our teeth, flex our psychic muscles, reward ourselves with a myriad of indulgences, and cheerfully fail.

What would work? How would we make changes ourselves or empower others to make changes? By persuading with right brain language to make one small symbolic change. If I stop being impatient in one small symbolic area, I will ultimately change an entire attitude, because in a holistic framework, when you change one part, you change the whole.

I have been explaining the right brain in our usual left brain way. Now we'll switch to a right brain mode.

Once a young man went to a Zen master and asked him for help. He told the master that his life was a shambles: he lived in a terrible home, he couldn't seem to change his life. The master listened carefully, went to see his house and agreed that everything was a mess. The master said there was nothing he could tell him or any exercise he could recommend, but he did want to give him a gift. The next day a beautiful couch was delivered to his disreputable home. The disconsolate young man didn't understand the gift, but he put it up against one of the dirty walls. A few days later, he was struck by how bad the wall looked in comparison with the beautiful couch, so he fixed up the wall to have a fitting exterior. You know the end of the story. First the exterior, then the yard, then the block, then the district, the city and finally the world were all made more attractive.

The story is about the way changes are made and is in the mode of change language. We are more apt to change our life from this story than from an explanation of how holistic thought works.

The power language of the right brain operates in a significantly different way from the language of explanation and command. When we moralize, it works to the extent that people see things the way we do. This is fine when we are talking to our friends, a select few whose views we share. We tell people who are already motivated to do something they already think they ought to, and, sure enough, they do it. All we have to be is clear. People usually give simple, trite explanations for their conversions. They say things like: "For the first time in my life, I realized that God loves me." They knew that from the Baltimore Catechism or the Gospel of John, and any preacher would be justified in complaining: "Why did it take twenty years for him to understand that when I've been saying that every week?"

Most pieces of information do not compel change. Information can be interpreted enough to squeeze it into our existing framework. Conversion happens when we keep our old information but change the framework. Then we see with new eyes and reinterpret all the old data, often at once, often over a period of time. When Paul experienced Jesus on the road to Damascus, he rearranged but kept a lifetime of rabbinic learning.

Look at the way Jesus treated the lawyer in Chapter 10 of Luke. A lawyer stood up to put him to the test: "Teacher, what shall I do to inherit eternal life?" Jesus answered with a question. "What is written in the law? How do you read it?" The lawyer replied: "You shall love the Lord your God with all your heart, and with all your soul, and with all your mind, and your neighbor as yourself. Jesus said, "You've got it right. Do that." End of discussion.

But the lawyer wished to justify himself, as the Scripture passage notes. He didn't want conversion. He wanted approval of the way he was.

Legal training is left-brain. We don't normally associate jokes, puns, poetry or stories with legal language, then or now. Notice, Jesus will not engage in a legal discussion of how close a person has to live or what qualifications he must possess to be considered a real neighbor. He doesn't define or clarify the text. Instead he tells the story of the good Samaritan we all know.

Why? What does Jesus do when he starts telling the story? First, he switches hemispheres. He changes the lawyer's point of view by giving him what John Shea calls the "view from the ditch." He leaves the law intact; he doesn't alter any line or introduce any further exegesis or form criticism. He just changes the roles and the point of view of the whole law. What would happen to our welfare laws if the people making the laws had the view from the waiting room or unemployment line?

The folks in the waiting room wouldn't add much new data but their whole approach would be radically different. If you ask people whom they have an obligation to help, you get one answer and one attitude. If you ask them who is eligible to help them, you get a different answer and a correspondingly different attitude.

That's what Jesus did to the lawyer. By altering his point of view from helper to helpless he effectively lured him to rethinking the whole law.

From this brief explanation flow several suggestions on how to use the findings of these right brain discoveries in preaching.

First, recognize the power of metaphorical language, of puns, jokes, sayings, double meanings and such. Watzlawick says, for example, that the slogan of the National Rifle Association, "When guns are outlawed, only outlaws will have guns," is technically a double bind, but it has enormous power. If a person has that on a bumper sticker, don't bother to argue. (He may be armed, besides.) Rather than meet such a position logically, without power, get your own bumper sticker that says, "Sell handguns! You could make a killing." That's not logical, but it is persuasive.

Recognize that nagging doesn't work. Neither does moralizing. You can moralize some people into doing more of the good they're already doing, and that will keep you coming back for more mistakes, but realize that your success is severely limited with any sentence that begins "So, therefore, let us . . ."

For a closer examination of nagging's futility, just reflect on the case of the tobacco companies vs. the surgeon general. Cigarette smoking kills people all the time. The facts are really not disputed. The surgeon general, most likely a left brain administrative type, thought that he would counteract the advertisers by making them put information about the health danger on all the ads. The tobacco company, on their part, would be able to continue to advertise. It is a clear case of hemisphere to hemisphere combat. It is information vs. impression. Beautiful people or scenes vs. the surgeon general's warning. No contest. The ads work as well as they ever did, and the expensive advertising still pays off. The lesson, repeated innumerable times on television, in magazines and on billboards, is that people act on symbols, impressions and implicit promises more than they do on unadorned data.

If you're looking for a rationale to spend money on art for your church, especially for the liturgy, you've just found one. Our almost exclusive left brain education is probably to blame for the predominance of poor art in our churches.

Second, besides recognizing metaphorical and story language's power, realize that you can destroy the power of stories and parables by explaining them. When you explain parables or symbols, you transfer the information to the left hemisphere where it is impotent. When you use Bible stories or aphorisms, realize that you can destroy them by explanation. Treat stories as patterns to be repeated, not explained.

Third, music stimulates the right brain. The allegiance of many people, both Catholics and Protestants alike, is in direct proportion to the quality and quantity of music they heard and sang, especially while young.

Beware of what might be called a new form of "white lung disease." After too many years in a classroom the chalk dust gets into your lungs and you begin to view the whole world as a classroom. This is accompanied by an uncontrollable desire to explain and teach. The only cure for this is to develop an appreciation of the power of poetry and music.

Finally, learn to recognize stories acted out but not written down. The biblical stories are heuristic—they establish patterns of God's activity and human response that are still going on all over. The job of the preacher of power is to recognize and disseminate the recognition of the patterns of God's activity. The preacher's job is to read the story of the prodigal son and find that same pattern in the lives of the people in the audience. Once the people get a feel for the pattern, then the pattern interprets and shapes the raw experience of their life.

The preacher's goal is not to provide new data, but a fresh revelatory interpretation of existing data—the experience of the audience. The rearranging of interpretive patterns is best done with right brain language.

Right brain language is difficult to master and leaves the preacher open to criticism for lack of content and the presence of confusion. Let a powerful preacher say why he used so many literary artifices: "I must leave chaos within myself to give birth to a dancing star" (Nietzsche, in *Thus Spake Zarathustra*).

Part III

Action

TO LIVE THE WORD WITH LITTLE FOLKS

Francis T. Cancro

> Rev. Francis T. Cancro, a Philadelphia native, is a priest of the diocese of Charlotte, North Carolina. He is director of communications for his diocese, pastors the Bishop McGuinness High School community, and works as well in St. Leo's Parish in Winston-Salem. Before entering the priesthood he had a successful career in clowning, and this included both circus work and television. Father Cancro seemed the ideal person for a chapter on communicating with children.

Children are people. Like all other people in parish communities they present specific needs when confronted with the word of God in their lives. What I want to attempt here is not a series of skeletal services that a preacher can plug into any given Sunday, but rather a variety of ideas about the ministry of the word with children, looking at their special needs (physical and spiritual) and the Church's response to them. Children deserve more than shorter words and cute gimmicks to attract their attention during an otherwise grown-up Sunday experience. They deserve a theology that attempts to define who they are in this mix of pilgrims who journey to the Kingdom. They deserve leadership that recognizes their unique place in and contribution to the community of faith.

Before we can ask the question "How do I celebrate with children?" we have to ask the question "Who are these children I am celebrating with?" and "Who am I who breaks God's abiding word with them?" These vital questions help the preacher and minister of sacraments to recognize the unique fibre that this part of the parish community contributes to the over-all fabric of faith.

With the above-mentioned sensitivity there are a number of practical considerations to keep in mind when gathering to pray and preach with little ones. *The Directory for Masses with Chil-*

dren (n. 24) states that not everyone can preach to children. It gives the faculty to priest celebrants to allow others to preach when their relationship to a congregation of youngsters will allow them to communicate the word with greater ease. This statement can be the biggest godsend or the greatest copout. Many men in the pulpit readily turn this task over to others because they have never tried, or they feel uncomfortable with the prospect of children in their audience. Although not everyone can ultimately break the word with children, everyone can at least try. The things that I am about to propose are some helps for the seasoned preacher as well as for the beginner. Hopefully they can assist you in preparing and planning to take an initial risk or hone already established skills. Celebrants are called to an honest assessment of themselves as preacher and prayer leader when they are called to be so in a community of innocent, open and simple little folk.

The celebrant must also be aware of time and timing. Children tend to shift in their seats when too much time is taken with things insignificant to them. Celebrations with children have to be based on a system of planning that does more than pick songs and color schemes. Masses with children have to be planned with a sense of *timing* in all its component parts. Which are the most important rites? How are they to be emphasized? What elements can be done in a simpler style, at a faster pace? All these questions are good ones to have at hand when planning. We have fallen into the "group syndrome" at children's liturgies. We involve as many kids with as many tasks as we can. There is little regard for the time it takes. Ten different children read separate petitions at the prayer of the faithful and twenty more join in the procession at the presentation of gifts. Although from time to time these activities and the involvement of many are meaningful, they are not always. We sometimes sacrifice a central point or a sacred moment with children because our priorities of involvement and activity are more important than a discernment of what *should* be celebrated. Mass can be just as meaningful when the table is set beforehand and the petitions are presented in simpler formats. Kids will sit for over an hour if the *timing* of their worship—your actions and your words—involves them. We can learn much from the timed antics of the circus and the various shows-on-ice. These performers know that a child's attention can only be held by specific activities for short periods of time. They are also aware that the rapid succession of skits or attractions performed at varying pace is most effective in keeping a child mystified and absorbed for as long as a two hour performance. Kindergarten and first grade teachers could prove to be tremendous resource persons for your homily preparation and your parish liturgy teams.

Celebrants also have to learn to be faithful. This faithfulness is two-sided: a faithfulness to the children who have gathered to celebrate and a faithfulness to the word that lives in the Church. Oftentimes people will come away hearing different things in a sermon because the themes or primary points of a sermon have hit them in different parts of their lives. Have you ever been to a child's Christmas celebration? Lately they've become birthday parties for Jesus—a nice touch and sometimes well put together—but do children *really* associate Christmas with a birthday? It seems to me that opening presents and gathering with families and the other *real* things that happen at Christmas are what they are excited about and immersed in. Sometimes we are not faithful to them because we mix up their symbols and fuzz up their images of great days. We do just the opposite with a feast like All Saints Day. It is a day for costumes and all else that the child's triduum of Halloween through All Souls should be! Sometimes we are not faithful to the Church which already has a problem with adults who see Christmas still as a birthday remembrance without a clue to what incarnation means, who see saints as stuffy parts of Christian history who do not touch the ordinary hopes and dreams of us who live on the other side of the Kingdom. Being faithful to all this is hard. I think that we lose the attentiveness of children because we are not faithful to a child's perception of the celebration.

Much more can be gained by working from their starting point instead of trying to get them to ours. To be faithful to all this means we have to ask the children themselves what their perceptions are or learn from parents and teachers (whose perception is keen) what a child focuses on when a day like Easter or a special Sunday parable rolls around.

A child's perception is usually not as sophisticated as our own. We see things with a logical or at least time-tested bent that is simply not part of a child's understanding. I remember visiting a friend who was hospitalized for abdominal surgery. Post-operatively the whole family joined around the bedside, and before they left for home they shared prayer. A young granddaughter had been allowed to visit. When her turn came to pray, she closed her eyes and fervently said, "O God, please take care of Grandma 'cause she has strings holding her tummy together." Simplicity in our own approach to the world and our faith would be a treasured gift to recapture! Such a gift can open our sensitivities if we are willing to pick apart and lay down our adult pretensions and see Easter eggs instead of Easter triduums or imaginative costumes instead of stale lists of white-robed martyrs.

A devastating experience for clowns is the approach of a child who shakes his head and says: "You're not a real clown." It happened in my own clowning experience when I started out, and I suspect it happens to most other young performing clowns. Usually the reason a child comes up with such a halting statement is that the clown has chosen either to simply act silly or to apply some learned and polished walk-around or other spoof. The clown in so doing has let go of his or her commitment to faithfulness in mirroring the small life encountered and allowing that child to laugh at his own childishness. In the world of the circus it is well known that children know when you are not faithful. And for the clown, when you are not faithful you are not funny. You are not real. And for the Church . . .?

Probably one of the hardest things to remember about worship with children is that you have to be an adult when you preach or pray with them. Sermonizing with young folks can lend itself to language that is more silly than simple. Although the use of visual aids or vibrant storytelling is an important element in children's worship, you should remember to be an *adult* storyteller weaving stories for children. Don't be a child yourself. Children don't need another child in their midst; rather they need a leader and a guide through the experience of the word. They need someone who has seen what they see and can tell them the "who" and the "why" of it.

Presiding with children requires the ability to be trusted. That trust comes by the way you carry yourself, by the way you pick and use your words, and by the way you allow children to see you as a fellow pilgrim who has walked the same road they have, but for just a while longer. There are some very symbolic ways in which this trust can be built or strengthened in worship. Don't be pretentious. Rediscover the child now grown up inside of you. Be close to your worshipers. If you are six feet tall and they are three, you may have to adjust your level from time to time so that all the adult things connected to relationship and trust (eye contact, physical closeness, removal of threatening space) can also take hold with the children. Be aware of things like the force of your voice. Does it overpower them? Does it tantalize them to want to hear more? Be aware of what you are wearing. Is it too formal and crisp? Is it so loud and color-ridden that it distracts them from you? Be aware of your environment. Will they be lost beneath the pew tops in a dimly lighted rectangular church? Will they get lost in a vast and sterile sanctuary space that reminds them more of a gym floor? Trust comes from a closeness that is verbal, physical and comfortable.

I used to live in a parish that had a small staff and not a tremendous amount of space. Once each month the children of the parish gathered upstairs in the gym to celebrate the word and join their parents downstairs in the church at the presentation of gifts.

The worship generally included song, story, prayer and a group activity. The first noticeable thing about such a gathering is that sizes, shapes and *ages* vary in a gathering of children. A successful key to planning with children is to be aware of that. I know a ten year old who will argue for hours that he is no longer a kid. Your own experience must have taught you early on that one of the most important goals of childhood is to pass that imaginary line that separates little kids from older children. Older children resent any implication that they are little. That needs to be respected in worship. Often it is hard because of time and space limitations—you can't have a Sunday just for eight year olds! I have found that wonders can be worked when older children can gather for the same worship as younger children but share different responsibilities in that worship experience. Bigger kids make great helpers, especially if you are going to form a procession or do a skit. They can help a minister with an activity by guiding younger children through cutting and pasting or even praying. Use the talents and skills that your community of children exhibits. We are quick to run after adults to chair some group or minister in some way to the larger community. We should be as quick to identify and affirm the various gifts that individual children and their levels of development offer. The only concern is one that would call the minister to be realistic. What are the "best" age groups to work with? When do kids stop being kids? Pre-teens and adolescents have different worship needs. The types of stories you tell and the manner of your delivery as well as all the attendant prayer and song of worship will have to be different for them. Choose your age groups wisely. I have found ages four through ten a good working block. Under four you are emotionally babysitting. A good nursery program with Bible stories and activities might serve this set best. From eleven through fourteen there is a completely different identity, and that should be respected at prayer.

There are countless resources available to spark all sorts of ideas for special themes to celebrate with children. Don't be afraid to be creative with your words and your actions. Do be careful and sensitive about the use of your talents and their limitations.

Once upon a time there was a pastor who picked up a book that promised hundreds of ideas for homilies with children. The pastor happened upon a celebration that included the use of puppets (handmade, of course). Being a bold soul he memorized the script, practiced in front of a mirror, and on the day of the celebration geared himself up for what was guaranteed to be a great event. During the Mass, one of the puppets slipped off his hand and he confused his voice so that the boy talked like he girl puppet and vice versa. The children were more entertained by his noticeable uneasiness than by the puppets he was trying to use. He lived happily ever after—but the puppets were never heard from again.

Sometimes the use of props can be a great boost. The list is only as short as your creativity allows. Puppets, slides, balloons, juggling balls, stuffed animals, pictures, sounds and magic can do great things to drive a point home. Again, you are limited by your creativity but you have to know your limitations. Sometimes props fail because it is simply not *your* prop. In preparing to preach to children you cannot escape having to spend some time discovering yourself. I can tranform a paper bag and some cotton balls into sheep ears and hooves to speak about the Good Shepherd with a wool-sided perspective. I know others who are too sheepish (sorry) to attempt it. I have a friend who can dress up in raincoat and hat, put on fishing boots and carry a rod. Adding a Jewish accent transforms him into Peter the fisherman-apostle in a spellbinding way. I cannot. Gimmicks will only work if you can work the gimmicks. Some people have overdone them and others are still too afraid to try. If you're honest with yourself you may find a whole new world of images unfolding for you.

What I have tried to stress here is the fact that for the preacher, sermonizing to children is more than a skill. If one is to effectively proclaim the word to young people, then he must start by recognizing that the preaching ministry he immerses himself in goes beyond planning books. Preaching the word to children is a lifestyle. Be honest in assessing how you live the word in your own words. That honesty, coupled with a concern for timing, faithfulness, responsibility, trust and creativity, will make you a better minister in relationship to children. I have found this five-fold challenge a great help in my own rediscovery of God's word that I break and share with others—big and small—as we wind our way home.

HOW TO PREACH TO ADOLESCENTS

Kieran Sawyer, S.S.N.D.

> Sister Kieran Sawyer, S.S.N.D. holds degrees in English, theology and religious education. An experienced teacher and minister to youth, she conducts workshops throughout the country with emphasis on developing faith experiences for the young. She directs "The Tyme Out Youth Ministry Center" in Milwaukee, Wisconsin and is the author of several articles as well as *Developing Faith* and *Confirming Faith* (both Ave Maria Press). Her ministry and her proven talents prompted us to ask her to give the preacher some help in reaching teens.

My first response to the question how to preach to teens is "Don't!" Preaching, as the word is used by adolescents, names something done by angry parents, boring teachers, and long-winded pastors. No teen wants to be preached to (or at), and few will listen to or be much affected by preaching. The problem with preaching, as the word is understood by teens, is that it is an entirely one-sided form of discourse. The preacher has a message to convey, but, for whatever reason, the preachee doesn't want to hear it. Even though words are spoken, often in great amplitude, no real communication takes place.

Preaching, then, is decidedly not the best form of discourse for bringing the Christian message to adolescents. Let's try a second term. If we shouldn't preach to teens, perhaps we should use our preaching time to *teach* them. Teaching, a definite improvement over preaching, is the process of conveying information from one who has it to one who lacks and wants it. Many young people today sense that they lack clear knowledge of their faith and really want to be taught about it. They are usually open to a brief, interesting explanation of some aspect of Christianity or Catholicism—e.g., why bread and wine are used in the Eucharist, how reconciliation has changed over the centuries, what the Church actually teaches regarding nuclear war.

But teaching is largely an intellectual process. A person can understand a point of doctrine without being moved to deeper faith. Something more than teaching is needed if young people are to be helped to really grow as Christians. What we want is a form of communication that will really *reach* teens with the message of Christianity. How do we touch their hearts with the Gospel? How do we speak the truth so that they will really hear it and pattern their lives according to its challenges?

I will present some basic principles to follow in preparing homilies and other religious talks for teens. Then I will give concrete examples that put the principles into action. Several principles are combined in the various examples.

First Principle. Get as physically close to your audience as you can. In order to reach teens with your words, you need to be making eye-to-eye contact with them.

Second Principle. Bring the word itself alive. Reading Scripture is only one way of communicating it. The good news can also be told, or paraphrased, or signed, or sung, or danced, or dramatized, or mimed, or projected on a screen. None of this has to be elaborate, but teens, like the rest of us, are too familiar with the Scripture and need to be teased into listening to it with new ears.

Third Principle. Relate the Gospel to the world the teens know as real. Use examples from their daily lives, from last night's newspaper, from the movies and TV shows they watch, from the music they listen to.

Fourth Principle. Use language that has meaning in the everyday world of youth. This doesn't mean that you have to be up on the latest teenage jargon (an impossible task, since last month's *in* words are already *out*), but you should avoid concepts that are too abstract and "churchy." I recently heard someone ask a group of teens, "What graces have you received from the Holy Spirit this week?" Most teens I know would have no idea how to answer such a question. Those words simply don't name reality as they experience it.

Fifth Principle. Involve your audience in your message. Call for an immediate physical or oral response to what you have just said. This is one of the best ways of capturing their attention and helping them to think with you about the message.

Sixth Principle. Presume the good will of your young audience. Many adults are defensive and negative in the presence of teens. They unconsciously attribute to this group of young people all the bad things they have heard and read about teens in general. It is much more likely that you are talking to a group of adolescents who have positive attitudes, sound values, searching minds, and deep faith. Speak to them as if these things are true, and you will find them to be so.

SOME EXAMPLES

Movable Chairs. Getting close to your group can be accomplished in several ways. If they are spread out in a hall on individual chairs, ask them to pick up their chairs and move as close to you as possible. If they are scattered throughout a large church, ask everyone to move to the front six pews, or invite them all to sit on the floor in the sanctuary. If they must stay in pews or straight rows, *you* move—take your mike and walk down among the group. Another option which has worked effectively for me is to invite a panel of six or eight young people to come to the front as my respondents. I dialogue with the panel as a way of providing youth input and feedback during my talk.

Acting the Story. Dramatizing Scripture is an excellent way to bring new life to the old story. For example, before reading the Gospel of the sower and the seed (Mk 4:1–20) ask for some "hammy" volunteers to help you act it out. Assign the roles: the seed on the path, the seed in the thorns, the seed on the rocks, the good seed, the bird, the thorns. As you read the story from Scripture, your cast dramatizes the action: one "seed" gets carried off by the "bird," one shoots up fast and then withers, one is choked by the ugly "thorns" that grow up around it, three "seeds" flex their muscles as a sign of growth. When you read the second half of this passage, Jesus' explanation of the parable, the cast simply repeats the action, and your audience will repeat its appreciative laughter.

Telling the Story. I once participated in an evening Mass with a group of forty junior boys on retreat. When it was time for the Gospel, the celebrant asked if anyone could remember the story of the prodigal son well enough to tell it. One boy volunteered and gave a delightful rendition of this ancient story of God's love, complete with his own expansions. Since then I've often asked teens to *tell* Scripture rather than read it. Sometimes I ask for a particular story to be told; sometimes I ask several people to tell us their favorite story and explain what it means to them.

Reading in Parts. Any Scripture account that contains dialogue should be read by several readers, a narrator and a reader for each dialogue part. We're accustomed to seeing the passion read this way, but even there more roles could be added to get as many people involved as possible. I recently attended a Mass for the deaf during which the story of Abraham bargaining with God for the city of Sodom (Gen 18) was signed by two deaf people, one playing Abraham, the other, God. The sign language added a powerful dimension to the meaning of the story.

You Are There. Ask your group to enter into the story you are about to read and to imagine how *they* would have acted if they had been there. This works well, for instance, for the story of Peter walking on the water (Mt 14:22–33). After the reading, ask all present to decide how they would have responded to the invitation to walk on the stormy water. Say: "Raise your hand if you would have asked John to go first; if you would have climbed under the seat; if you would have told Jesus you were only kidding; if you would have trusted enough to walk toward Jesus." (Adapted from pp. 38–39 of *Movin' On* by Lyman Coleman, Serendipity House, 1976.) Then give some examples of the kinds of troubled waters Jesus asks us to walk over in real life: "You've had a fight with a friend. Jesus asks you to go through the trouble of apologizing and making up. Can you trust enough to do that?" "You didn't study for a test. Jesus asks you to face the trouble of a low grade rather than get the answers dishonestly. Can you keep your eyes on Jesus and off your friend's answers?" "You've done something that will make your parents angry. Jesus asks you to face the rough waters of telling them the truth rather than lie out of it. Can you do that for him?"

The Prophet Is You. Read 1 Samuel 3:1–19, the passage in which God calls young Samuel and gives him a message to take to Eli. Then say: "Suppose God spoke to you in the night and told you to carry a message to your family. He might say, 'Tell your family I am pleased with them because . . .' or 'Tell them I am displeased about . . .' What would he be pleased with? Displeased with?" Allow the group time to think about the message God would ask them to take to their families; then ask them to think about what message he might have for their friends, their school, their workplace, their athletic team, etc.

Thumbs Up, Thumbs Down. You want to talk to your group about the presence of God in their lives. They will need help in thinking about something so mysterious and wonderful. Say: "God has a problem getting through to us human beings, but he keeps on trying. It's almost like a reverse game of hide and seek; God wants us to find him hiding in our world, and we keep trying not to look too hard. I'm going to explain some of the places where God can be found. You tell us with your thumb if you find God there. Thumbs up means "Yes," thumbs down,

"No," thumb sideways "So so." Some people find God in nature—beautiful sunsets, wild storms, new fallen snow. Do *you* find God in nature? Show us with your thumb." Continue with similar examples of God's presence: in family life, church, moral decisions, love relationships, birth, death, trouble, etc. Ask for the thumb response after each.

Stand If. Sometimes you need a full-body response to wake a group up. I've used this activity to introduce a talk on the importance of the Eucharist. I begin with a list of statements the group will enjoy responding to: "Stand if you think teachers give too much homework. Remain standing if you do it all. Stand if you've never been spanked. Stand if you've ever had a traffic ticket. Stand if your parents trust you. Remain standing if they *should* trust you."

Then switch to statements on the Eucharist like these: "Stand if you really listen to the sermon on Sunday. Stand if you ever told the pastor you liked his homily, or didn't like it. Stand if you go to Mass with your family. Remain standing if you go willingly. Stand if you know what transubstantiation means. Stand if you ever invited a Protestant friend to Mass with you. Stand if you understand the Mass well enough to explain it to a Buddhist friend who doesn't know about Jesus."

Buzz Partner. Ask the teens to talk about some point or question with the person sitting next to them. For example: "Tell your partner about a teenager you admire, about something you are afraid of, about something you hope to accomplish, about a fault you are trying to correct." Or: "When was the last time you told your mom you loved her? The last time you lied to her? The last time you offered to help her with something?" Or: "Tell your partner three words that describe the *you* your friends know, the *you* your parents know, the *you* your little brothers and sisters know, the *you* your teachers know."

Sharing the Word. Select several Scripture passages that you want your group to think about—for instance, passages that record God's promises to his people (e.g., Rom 8:28; Is 40:31; Mt 7:7; Rev 3:20; Jn 14:23; Mt 28:20; 2 Cor 9:8; Phil 1:6). Type these on a handout sheet or project them on an overhead projector. Present each passage and allow the group time to think about it. Then ask them to select the passage that contains the promise they most need to hear from God today. Ask them to tell the person next to them which passage they selected and why.

Rating Scale. Present a scriptural ideal and ask your listeners to measure their own lives against that ideal. For example, read Romans 12:9–21. Then take each phrase of the epistle and say: "Paul tells us that we must love one another sincerely. On a 1 to 10 scale, rate your sincerity in dealing with your friends, your family. Paul tells us to prefer good over evil. Rate your desire to do what God wants and to avoid the things that displease him." A rating like this can be done silently in one's own heart, or, in an intimate retreat-type setting, it can be shared with a partner or small group. (This rating exercise can be found in *Breaker 1–9* by Lyman Coleman, Serendipity House, 1976.)

Music. A musical number can often be used as a starting point for a homily or for the homily itself. For example, David Meece's "Give Me Just a Little More Time" is a plea from God to let him into our busy worlds. The song can be used to help teens think about their priorities and the amount of time they spend deepening their relationship with God. (This song and other helpful numbers are found on the album *Are You Ready?*—Word Incorporated, Waco, Texas.) The teens' own popular music often contains messages that can be used as attention-getters for homilies. An invaluable resource for keeping you abreast of what is good and bad in youth music is a monthly cassette tape produced by disc jockey Father Don Kimball (Cornerstone Media, Inc., Box 6236, Santa Rosa, Cal. 95406).

Attention-Getters. A true-life story, a newspaper account, a well-known novel, or a popular TV show or movie can easily be the starting point for reaching youth with the message. For example, I recently heard someone use the story of "E.T." to explain the mystery of the incarnation. I myself have used Jem and Scout's discovery of the real Boo Radley (in the novel *To Kill a Mockingbird*) to help young people to understand the various ways they come to discover God. (This lesson can be found on the cassette tape "Does Johnny Believe?"—Ave Maria Press, 1978.) Youth Specialties publishes a book called *Tension Getters* which contains sixty-eight real-life problems and predicaments for today's youth. Each is presented in a catchy paragraph and followed by related Scripture references.

CONCLUSION

The ideas presented in this article have all been used effectively in various settings with groups of teens. Many if not all of them would probably be equally effective in a gathering made up of both adults and youth. I would encourage all parish homilists to focus on their teenaged parishioners often, at least one Mass each weekend, or at all Masses at least once a month. The hearts of teenagers are fertile soil, ready for the word of God. It is up to us to find ways to *reach* them with that word.

BIBLIOGRAPHY

Besides the resources mentioned in the article, the following books contain excellent ideas that can be adapted to fit the preaching situation.

The Sharing Program
by Tom Zanzig
St. Mary's Press
Winona, Minn. 55987

Values Clarification
by Simon, Howe, and Kirschenbaum
Hart Publishing Co.
New York, N.Y. 10012

Ideas published quarterly
Youth Specialties
1224 Greenfield Drive
El Cajon, Cal. 92021

Encyclopedia of Serendipity by Lyman Coleman—and other Serendipity books
Serendipity House
Box 1012
Littleton, Col. 80160

Developing Faith and Confirming Faith
by Kieran Sawyer, S.S.N.D.
Ave Maria Press
Notre Dame, Ind. 46556

Creative Resources for Youth Ministry (series of six books)
by Rice, Roberto, and Yaconelli
St. Mary's Press
Winona, Minn. 55987

PREACHING TO THE LIVING AT A FUNERAL

Charles Hudson

> Rev. Charles Hudson was ordained for the Archdiocese of Newark, N.J. twenty-three years ago and has spent all but five of those years in hospital work. He is director of pastoral care at St. Elizabeth Hospital in Elizabeth, N.J. and has become a strong advocate for the hospice movement. He helped found "Center for Hope," a free-standing hospice program caring for the terminally ill and their families. His ministry, combined with exceptional preaching talent, prompts many people to request his presence at funerals. He was a logical choice for sharing insights on this kind of preaching.

"Ever since mom died and after having experienced all that I did through the wake and funeral, I now find myself talking differently to those of my people who come to me with their sorrow and pain." This comment was made to me during a recent conversation I had with a brother priest who had recently lost his mother after a long and painful illness. When I asked him to elaborate, he went on to say that he knew somehow that he had been changed, that his mother's death had left him with many feelings he had not yet sifted through—feelings which enabled him to relate differently to others.

Robert Browning Hamilton expressed similar thoughts in one of his poems:

> I walked a mile with Pleasure.
> She chattered all the way
> But left me none the wiser
> For all she had to say.
>
> I walked a mile with Sorrow
> and ne'er a word said she;

> But oh, the things I learned from her
> When Sorrow walked with me.

Once you have walked with sorrow in your own life, you are never the same. In some way you become shaped by the effect that sorrow has had on you. Someone once said that you either become a better or a bitter person. What one learns through the experience of grief and the struggles to survive is translated and expressed to others in both verbal and non-verbal language. What you have personally experienced in your life in terms of separation, loss and death will no doubt have the greatest influence on you when it comes time to make a sensitive response to others in their time of grief and sorrow. Your empathetic response to others will flow from the memory of what you needed and received at the time when you sustained the blow of a significant loss. You will more readily recognize those very same emotions and feelings because you once stood where those before you now stand. The meaning of what you say to others is not in the words you speak but they are in you.

It is so very important to realize that there are many experiences of loss happening in our lives that leave us with the need to grieve. Death, which is in many instances the ultimate and final loss, is often seen as occurring at the end of a person's life. Yet we encounter the impact of death in our lives often without realizing it. Life has woven through it a series of endings and new beginnings, with the endings accompanied by feelings similar to those we experience at the time of death. A relationship that has meaning to us suddenly and unexpectedly ends and we face the painful task of accepting the void created by the separation; we lose contact with people, places or objects in which we have invested significant parts of ourselves; intimacy with another is abruptly diminished because a confidence is broken. These are just a few examples of moments when we feel the impact of death upon ourselves. It is crucial to our capacity to relate to other people who come to us with broken hearts for us to accept our own feelings. Very often I have found that our hesitancy to deal with what is now happening inside another is because we have not adequately dealt with what has happened inside ourselves. We then become uncomfortable with what another is expressing and we begin to distance ourselves from them. Instead of an empathetic presence, they will often come to interpret our distancing as rejection, thus intensifying their feeling of isolation and loneliness.

As we begin to look out from ourselves to focus on the family as survivors, we must be sensitive to the emotions that well up inside them. We should be able to identify and recognize those emotions and through our acceptance of them help the survivor to identify, recognize and accept them. In most instances, people will not be affected by the words that we offer as much as what we become to them in this moment of crisis. They will for the most part be stunned, in shock or just confused and not be able to truly take in all that we say. Therefore it is usually futile to attempt to explain why it all happened even though they may be asking the question why. They want only one thing and one thing only—to be consoled by someone who understands and accepts where they are at this time of loss.

The funeral rite and the homily must give to those present a sense of hope based on faith and what we believe without denying them the importance of grieving and weeping because of what they have lost and will not have again in this life. Basically, we could say that grief is mourning the lost parts of ourselves we invested in the person we have lost. We weep and mourn, not so much for the dead person as for ourselves and for what the death of this person will mean to us in our struggle to survive. As one young girl said to her teacher after the death of her father, death meant to her a series of ''no mores''—no more Saturday morning breakfasts at McDonald's, no more camping trips, no more long walks on the beach searching for seashells. A part of ourselves that has been and a part of ourselves that will never be are often part of the mourning process in any funeral. One of the most powerful descriptions of the need to grieve comes from the Gospel account of the resurrection of Lazarus. The words of Scripture clearly describe how Jesus wept for his friend Lazarus even though he knew that Lazarus would soon be given life once again. It is extremely important in our ministering to the survivors that we give permission for them to take time to openly express their feelings. Often shock and denial, which have been described as the anesthesia of the human emotional system, prevent emotions from surfacing. Gradually the emotions do begin to come and they must be patiently encouraged, accepted and understood. If we are uncomfortable with expressions of grief that come from those we seek to comfort, then we should look within ourselves for the source of the discomfort. Those who attempt to stunt the emotional release in others are often treating themselves rather than being sensitive to the needs of those who have sustained the loss of a loved one.

Without fully realizing it, we could attempt to repress the feelings of the grief-stricken by talking about the death in abstract terms and negating the impact of the loss by emphasizing the spiritual dimension of the resurrection and life eternal. Ritual is an extremely important part of the process of healing that must begin with the funeral service. The funeral ritual is a place to deal with the grief. It is in this ritual that the loss is dealt with in human and spiritual terms. The funeral liturgy helps to actualize the reality of the fact that a death has taken place. It may seem strange, but before the survivors can begin the process of grief they must first admit and accept the fact that a death has happened, that the person is gone and will not be seen again in this life. The symbols we then use can become a source of hope as they point those present in the direction of faith and trust in a loving God.

I believe that people do not expect us to speak words to them that will lift their spirits above the immediate pain of loss. They do expect that the funeral ritual will have a ring of authenticity to it, that the individual who has died will be spoken of in terms that reflect the life he or she has lived. In preparing a homily for the liturgy, some effort should be made to collect information about the deceased. When my mother died several years ago, it was important that whatever was said at the Mass would accurately reflect my mother's life. Shortly before her death, one of my patients at the hospital gave me a small religious card on which was contained the following message: "On Calvary two types of courage were present—the courage to die and the courage to go on living." It was these simple few lines that I believe captured the essence of my mother's life. She had survived the death of my dad at a very young age and later the sudden and unexpected death of both my younger brothers. She possessed a courage deeply rooted in her faith which enabled her to face the task of going on living. When she came to the point of accepting her own death she did it with the same level of courage.

I wanted those present to leave the church that morning of the funeral with that final memory of her firmly planted in their memories. I believe that our people deserve no less when it comes time for them to participate in the funeral liturgy of their deceased loved ones. It is important that somehow they come away from the funeral with the comforting knowledge that the person really lived his or her life and had some very meaningful moments. Those meaningful moments can be then connected with and related to some of the meaningful moments that the Scriptures record for us from the life of Christ and the lives of those who were touched by him.

In order to speak with authenticity about the person who has died, a series of questions may be helpful when sitting down with the family. You may use these questions in any way you feel comfortable. All they are meant to do is provide some type of framework within which you can best prepare what you will say during the funeral liturgy.

What adjective would best describe the deceased? How did they best see themselves? (As a husband, a father, a son, a friend, a businessman? As a wife, a mother, a homemaker, a businesswoman, a friend?)

If you could name one value or lesson they most wanted to teach their children or the next generation, what would it be?

Was there any one achievement or accomplishment that would make their eyes light up when you mentioned it?

Was there any one achievement in which they took the greatest pride?

Did they ever put pictures or mottos on the office wall or on the kitchen refrigerator?

Was there anything to which they were opposed?

Was there any cause or movement that they felt deeply about and supported?

Did they consider themselves to be a Christian?

Were they active in church? If so, in what ways?

Did they have any favorite hymns or stories from Scripture?

If they would have me say one thing about them from the pulpit, what do you think it will be?

If they wished to leave one last thought for those attending this funeral service, what do you think it would be?

Because they lived, why is the world a better place?

I firmly believe that a funeral must not only declare that a life has ended, but, equally as important, declare that a life has been lived. The memory of that life is very much embedded in those who are grieving, and it is most helpful to the grief process to include those memories in a meaningful way in the words we express. The above questions may enable you to collect valuable insights into the life of the deceased person. These insights and examples can then be related to the Scripture readings or to some event or character contained in Scripture. At a recent funeral of a close friend, I used the example of salt to describe my friend. Jesus called us to become the salt of the earth. My friend was the salt that flavored and enhanced the experience of life for his family. His sense of humor, his philosophy and attitude toward life enriched the lives of those whom he loved. Such examples can help those present to visualize more clearly the activity of God in relation to the life of the dead person.

Authenticity is not the only important quality. Flexibility should also guide us in preparing a funeral liturgy that will prove consoling to those present. It has been said that relationships which do not end peacefully never end at all. Dr. Kübler Ross, in her writings and lectures on the dynamics of dying and death, often refers to the importance of dealing with the "unfinished business" that may exist between ourselves and those who are dying. Funerals, therefore, ought to be a place where some of what has not been resolved peacefully should be dealt with, so that those attempting to survive may do so with as little feeling of regret and guilt as possible. This was brought home forcefully to me at a recent funeral. The daughter of a woman, who had died unexpectedly, had written a letter to her mother which contained many of the feelings she had always intended to share but never got around to actually doing. It was part of the unfinished business that existed between her mother and herself. I invited her to read the letter as part of the liturgical celebration if she felt it would be helpful to her. After some thought and reflection, she read the letter at the end of the funeral liturgy. When I met her a few weeks later, she told me of how much it had meant to have been able to share her thoughts with all those who attended the funeral.

Experiences like that one have convinced me that it is good to invite the family and friends to plan the funeral Mass, choose the readings from Scripture or select certain hymns that have meaning for them. This kind of participation helps them derive even more comfort from the liturgy. After all is said and done, don't we do the same for ourselves when death has taken from us a significant person? The least we can offer to others is what we hope we will receive ourselves.

Perhaps Dr. Kübler Ross summed it all up best when she wrote the following in her book *Death: The Final Stage of Growth:*

> Death is the final stage of growth in this life. There is no total death. Only the body dies. The self or spirit or whatever you may wish to label it, is eternal. What is important is to realize that whether we understand fully why we are here or what will happen when we die, it is our purpose as human beings to grow—to look within ourselves to find and to build upon the source of peace and understanding and strength which is our inner selves, and to reach out to others with love, acceptance, patient guidance and hope for what we all may become together.

HAVE PATIENCE—
WE'LL BE IN ST. CROIX TONIGHT

John W. Conway

> Rev. John W. Conway is currently a hospital chaplain in the Archdiocese of Newark. He studied at Darlington Seminary and at the Catholic University of America, where he received a licentiate in sacred theology. While serving in parochial ministry, he also taught high school religion courses. Father Conway has lost count of the number of times he has been asked to celebrate nuptial Masses and to preach the wedding homily. His chapter on that topic offers practical advice, reasonable expectations and some humorous observations.

"Inasmuch as I have not been a parish priest, save for a single month decades ago, weddings are events at which I officiate only rarely (twice annually on an average) and for close friends. And yet experience taught me quite early that a nuptial homily has its own special problems. It dare not be long, especially within a Mass; it addresses a man and a woman at a uniquely intimate moment in their lives; it is delivered by a priest who ordinarily has not experienced the relationship that links this couple; and it should include a message to the congregation."

So says Walter J. Burghardt, S.J. in *Tell the Next Generation* (Paulist Press, 1980). This is a man of great intellect, a theologian who goes before and comes after Vatican II, a man whose homilies are extremely well thought out and chiseled grammatically, a priest who has been in touch with human nature and reflected deeply upon it.

My experience of Church has been different from his, but I agree totally with his four points. I do believe a wedding homily should be (1) short, (2) personal, (3) aware of the mystery that is marriage, and (4) addressed to the congregation beyond the wedding party.

For fifteen years I was a parish priest. As a teacher in a girls' high school, I was asked to officiate at about eighty five weddings a year. For the past ten years, as a hospital chaplain, I have watched—and listened to—many nurses entering marriage. And I have formed some opinions.

The first problem with the homily may well be out of your control—the reader of the Scriptures. I've listened to friends, uncles, godparents, brothers and baby sisters take on 1 Corinthians 13. Often enough they stammered, stuttered, wept, mumbled, and read with express-train speed in a monotone. They survived and can now return to the pew, from which they came. For them, it's over. For you, it begins.

How do you build on the text of an unheard reading?

I think of three possibilities. First, the *challenge*. In the planning stage, ask the couple whether the person they have chosen has had any experience with public reading. Hint at the difficulties and, if they begin to doubt, suggest alternatives. Second, the *rehearsal tryout*. Have the readers practice. Possibly with patience and repetition, you can correct the glaring errors. The drawback here is adding a half hour to the rehearsal and the knowledge that the tension of the wedding day will most likely undo all your practice. Third, the *rephrase*—perhaps the best solution. I often find myself saying, "As Harry/Joan read from St. Paul, 'If I speak with the tongues of men or angels . . .' " In this case, the congregation will hear at least part of the text you are trying to develop. It's hardly the perfect solution, but then maybe you wanted to deliver a sermon rather than a homily anyway.

Let us return to Father Burghardt's four points.

1. *Short*. Who listens? Who hears? I have watched many bridesmaids approach the altar with quivering bouquet, and ushers moving into the wrong pew. The maid of honor wants to take the bride's bouquet at the right moment, and the best man desires to produce the ring at the correct time. The bride and groom have

so many things on their minds. (Is the veil straight? Will the sun shine for photographs? Will we be on time for the reception? Will the honeymoon meet our expectations?)

Do the bride and groom hear the homily? I think not. Ask them after the fact. A devastating question! My ego is best preserved when the couple returns from the honeymoon and remarks, "What a great wedding!" It is destroyed when I ask, "Do you remember what I said?" The blank look, and the loving hand-squeeze, tell it all. I once officiated at the wedding of close friends. They were in their early thirties, mature. They planned the ceremony to the last detail. They chose articulate lectors and good musicians. They enjoyed the celebration. They smiled and nodded in agreement during the homily. Returning from the honeymoon, they asked, "What did you say in the homily?"

The most publicized wedding of our day was that of Prince Charles and Lady Diana. The archbishop of Canterbury preached a homily that lasted three minutes. I wonder what they remember of it. Three minutes. Yes, indeed, it should be short.

2. *Personal.* Here is one of the catches. Either you know them or you don't. It's great when they are family, friends, former students or parishioners whom you know. It is not that great when they are a couple you've never met before. The challenge here is to get to know them during the marriage preparation. Welcome them. Make them feel at ease. It's probably better if you talk with them in their own living room. (There's something comfortable about your own turf—and rectory offices are usually very official. And forbidding!) If you don't know them, find out who they are. What has been their experience of Church? Are they there because of their own faith commitment? Perhaps they want to please their parents? Maybe they don't know a judge. Nonetheless, they are at your door, and in love—and wanting to be married. At least we should find out who they are.

If you listen long enough, you will know who they are. If you come to know them and love them, you are ready to preach the homily at *their* wedding. Discover them both, reflect on the love of God, and speak from the heart—but briefly. Speak to them personally about who they are, what they do, and where they fit into the community. I'm tempted to give the same homily at every wedding. I've done it and continue to do it. But try to speak to their situation—this is a new and unique couple. (I can't always do it but I try.) I have in my possession the "collected sermons" of Fulton Sheen, Ronald Knox and Walter Burghardt, along with various homily services. They give me ideas. But I could never take one and preach it. It is not my style. Sheen is Sheen but you are you. You may never be as eloquent but you will be real.

3. *The Mystery That Is Marriage.* Of marriage, Paul said, "This is a great mystery." I'm sure he was not the first to have the idea—nor, indeed, the last. In spite of canon lawyers and liturgists, it continues; and so will it always. The canonists speak of "correct form." The liturgists hope for "sacramental celebration." As do I. But my reality tells me something different from the ideal. Face it, it's frequently messy.

You have before you two people who have clicked romantically, biologically and sexually. They come to this community to declare their intentions, to fulfill their desire to be together, to start a family, to hang on to each other. Common Marriage Preparation (to them) is usually un-romantic. "We have each other; isn't that enough?" (I'm delighted when they choose "Pre-Cana" or "Engaged Encounter." I rationalize that it gets the burden off my back.) Can twenty-five years of priesthood overcome the wisdom of a twenty year old in love?

The mystery that is marriage. I've seen some of my "best marriages" break up in divorce or annulment. So many of the ones that scared me seem to thrive. A mystery—to me, at least. Speak with love to this couple. But know that their reality is not yours—exactly. They may know something in the heart that is foreign to you. A mystery, indeed.

I was once at a wedding at which the groom read the following from the *Song of Solomon:* "How beautiful you are, my love, how beautiful you are! Your eyes, behind the veil, are doves. . . . Your lips are a scarlet thread and your words enchanting. . . . Your two breasts are two fawns, twins of a gazelle, that feed among the lilies. You are wholly beautiful, my love, and without a blemish."

The bride followed from the same book: "My beloved is fresh and ruddy, to be known among ten thousand. . . . His cheeks are beds of spices, banks sweetly scented. His lips are lilies, distilling pure myrrh. . . . His hands are golden, rounded, set with the jewels of Tarshish. His belly is a block of ivory covered with sapphires. His legs are alabaster columns set in sockets of pure gold. . . . His conversation is sweetness itself; he is altogether lovable."

I was attending, not officiating, at this one—thank God! I waited, with some glee, to see what the officiant would do with these readings. He ignored them! He spoke of the glories of union in Christ. But, as I watched this couple before the altar, I realized that their minds were set, not on union with Christ, but on union with each other. They had chosen *their* readings from Scripture. They spoke of eyes, lips, breasts, cheeks, bellies and legs. Perhaps, without knowing it, they spoke of incarnation.

The parents squirmed. The officiant ignored. But I think the couple were right on target. They wanted to discover and explore the other. Perhaps we are more comfortable with our theology than with their lived reality. There is a time when "good theology" must give way to this couple's individuality and sexuality. On this day, do you believe they can embrace our best sacramental theology?

We enter this day after months of preparation with gowns, bands, florists, caterers, menus and honeymoon plans. The bride's father has shelled out big money. It should not be this way—this pagan way—we cry. But it is. We want sanitized "union with Christ." They want rolling together on St. Croix. Who is right? I think both. Age fifty-one looks at twenty-one, and remembers. I want to scream, "I know more than you do." But, at that age, I would not have accepted; I would not have listened.

Many say that this is the best time to insist on the best readings, the best order, and the best music. But I wonder. Life is not always what we like. Some years ago, I received a most important bit of advice from Father Edward Price, now pastor of St. Genevieve's, Elizabeth, N.J. He said, "If you are good to people at the peak moments of their lives (baptisms, weddings, funerals), they will never forget you. If you are not, they will never forgive you." How right he was. Hospital chaplains meet the alienated. I guess ninety-four percent of them have had personality conflicts with the clergy—all silly things, stupid things, but real to the people involved. ("My mother-in-law had written this beautiful poem, but Father would not allow it." "I really wanted 'The First Time Ever I Saw Your Face' to be sung after the vows but Father thought 'Ave Maria' would be better.") I agree that Father had better taste but is this the best time to insist on it?

We live in a split world—the ideal and the real. The ideal demands that the wedding rehearsal start at 7 o'clock sharp, the wedding at 4 o'clock sharp, and the music be traditional, classical and good. The real world has the wedding party coming at 7:35—when you are due for a parish council meeting or wake at 7:45. The wedding begins at 4:25, and in the middle of it people begin arriving for the 5:15 parish Mass. Or worse, the U.S. Open comes on TV at 5 o'clock, and the couple really does like "The First Time . . ."

It's one more irritation for you, but a singular moment for them. If *you* are gracious, they will remember. Maybe—just maybe—this is the best homily you will preach that day. Our actions do speak louder than our words.

4. *A Message to the Community.* Take for granted that the wedding party is usually out of touch with reality. The mother of the bride is exhausted; the mother of the groom is excited; the fathers have mixed feelings. ("It's about time" or "Can he/she really be old enough?") However, the rest of the congregation usually listen to the homily. Who are they? They know one of the bridal pair. They are interested. I think you can reach them. They may not have been in church for a long time.

Bring warmth and enthusiasm. Everyone responds to those qualities. I think this is what Jesus did. They are usually married folk. They have been here and beyond. And they know. Their honeymoons are far in the past. Now it's diapers, Little League or driving to gymnastics; it's a troublesome teen-ager, a rebellious twenty year old. Real life; real problems. Their dreams have not turned out the way they imagined. Bring them the word of God.

Speak to them. They will be listening. They sit contemplating their own lives—and wanting encouragement. You/Jesus can speak a word to them. Say it.

Whenever I attend an ordination, certain thoughts come to mind—the youth of the new priests, their zeal and excitement, their total love, dedication and enthusiasm. It gets sidetracked for lots of us; we have been through it. But there are a number of older priests who are as dedicated and enthusiastic as when they were ordained. They show us what is possible, if we are willing to work at it. The young ones remind us of what we hoped to be.

I know the same is true at weddings. The married couples in the congregation will remember their day, and what happened to their ideals in the following years. They might not speak of it when they are cheering and throwing rice on the church steps, but if you ask them about their wedding as the reception progresses, they will usually tell you.

They will speak of the day itself—probably apocryphal by now. ("Helen was twenty-five minutes late"; "Joe got stuck in the snow"; "The ushers were so nervous that they pulled the runner before the first guest arrived.") With another glass of champagne, they might speak of the years of their marriage: what went right—and wrong.

Not for a minute do I believe that a wedding homily will reverse the patterns of a marriage. But I think you are given a chance to put some questions to the community. A majority of the weddings I've had settle for a reading of 1 Corinthians 13. If a good reader announces that "Love is always patient and kind . . . is never jealous. . . is not resentful . . . is always ready to excuse . . . and to endure whatever comes . . ." then the ball is in their (your/my) court.

I have my alibis—lots of them—to explain why St. Paul did not understand my situation (and why Jesus' teaching is a bit misguided in the twentieth century)! However, breaking into these excuses is the couple standing before us, and the seventy-five year old couple in the next pew who still love each other wildly. (They're there. A hospital chaplain sees them often.)

If you say a word about patience, resentfulness or jealousy, they will hear you. If you predict that the newlyweds will need forgiveness, they will understand. If you point out that Scripture frequently refers to the love of God for his people in terms of marriage—and indicate the couple before them (loving, forgiving, at pains to please and singular in affection)—they will probably be astonished. But that is the message.

And we need to hear it.

We come with our failures, mistakes, misunderstandings and errors in judgment. (Most do not come with malice.) But we hurt and have been hurt, and we lick our wounds. You have the opportunity to say to this community, "We have failed but let's go on from here." You have the opportunity to say to this couple, "You will fail, but arise, and go on from there."

A message to the community of which you are a part. Speak

to their reality the healing word of Jesus. Maybe you will touch one couple, one individual in this congregation. If so, count it a great success. Perhaps, if you are really lucky, *you* will hear what you've said. In that case, you will come alive—and the wedding homily will be a great success.

SUMMARY STATEMENT

Some people have the "Good Eye." They have a gift, a feel, a touch, an instinct others lack. They are astute and sensitive observers of life. This book brings some of them together in the hope that they will be of service to the preacher. They are priests, bishop, mother, professional storyteller, woman religious, Scripture scholar, hospice counselor, editor, retreat director, seminary professor and even former clown. They will help the preacher to speak not only of the divine story but of all those human stories so present in his world. They will help the preacher see what needs to be seen, and as a result know what needs to be said. Then the homily will evidence a feel for the pain, joy, doubt, fear, confusion and hope of those people gathered together to hear the word. They will be helped to make some sense of life and return to their homes and day to day struggles with more than the parish bulletin.